SHAMBHALA
CLASSICS

BOOKS BY THOMAS CLEARY

I CHING STUDIES

The Taoist I Ching, by Liu I-ming (1986)*
The Buddhist I Ching, by Chih-hsu Ou-i (1987)*
I Ching: The Tao of Organization, by Cheng Yi (1988)*
I Ching Mandalas: A Program of Study for The Book of Changes
    (1989)*

TAOIST STUDIES

The Inner Teachings of Taoism, by Chang Po-tuan (1986)*
Understanding Reality: A Taoist Alchemical Classic (1987)
The Art of War, by Sun Tzu (1988)*
Awakening to the Tao, by Liu I-ming (1988)*
The Book of Balance and Harmony (1989)
Immortal Sisters: Secrets of Taoist Women (1989)*
Mastering the Art of War, by Zhuge Liang & Liu Ji (1989)*
Back to Beginnings: Reflections on the Tao (1990)*
The Tao of Politics: Lessons of the Masters of Huainan (1990)*
Further Teachings of Lao-tzu: Understanding the Mysteries
    (1991)*
Vitality, Energy, Spirit: A Taoist Sourcebook (1991)*

BUDDHIST STUDIES

The Original Face (1978)
The Sayings and Doings of Pai-chang (1979)
Timeless Spring: A Soto Zen Anthology (1980)
Entry into the Inconceivable: An Introduction to Hua-yen
    Buddhism (1983)
The Flower Ornament Scripture, 3 vols. (1984–1987)*
Shobogenzo: Zen Essays by Dogen (1986)
Entry into the Realm of Reality: The Text (1989)*
Entry into the Realm of Reality: The Guide, by Li Tongxuan
    (1989)*
Zen Essence: The Science of Freedom (1989)*
Zen Lessons: The Art of Leadership (1989)*
Transmission of Light: Zen in the Art of Enlightenment,
    by Zen Master Keizan (1990)
The Blue Cliff Record (1992)*

*Published by Shambhala Publications

THE JAPANESE ART OF WAR

UNDERSTANDING THE CULTURE OF STRATEGY

THOMAS CLEARY

SHAMBHALA

BOSTON & LONDON

2005

Shambhala Publications, Inc.
Horticultural Hall
300 Massachusetts Avenue
Boston, Massachusetts 02115
www.shambhala.com

9 8 7 6 5 4 3 2 1
Printed in the United States of America
♾ This edition is printed on acid-free paper that meets
the American National Standards Institute Z39.48 Standard.
Distributed in the United States by Random House, Inc., and
in Canada by Random House of Canada Ltd

The Library of Congress catalogues the previous edition of this
work as follows:
Cleary, Thomas, F., 1949–
    The Japanese art of war: understanding the culture of strategy /
    Thomas Cleary.—1st ed.
        p. cm.
    ISBN 0-87773-907-2
    ISBN 0-87773-653-7 (pbk.)
    ISBN 1-59030-245-1 (Shambhala Classics)
    1. National characteristics, Japanese. 2. Bushido. 3. Japan—
Civilization. 4. Japan—History, Military. I. Title
DS830.C65 1991
952—dc20   90-52801   CIP

CONTENTS

THE JAPANESE ART OF WAR

INTRODUCTION

Use anger to throw them into disarray, use humility to make them
  haughty.
Tire them by flight, cause division among them.
Attack when they are unprepared, make your move when they do not
  expect it.
Be extremely subtle, even to the point of formlessness;
Be extremely mysterious, even to the point of soundlessness;
Thereby you can be the director of the opponent's fate.

SUN TZU, *THE ART OF WAR*

During one of the recent flareups of trade friction between the United
States and Japan, a prominent critic was complaining to a member of
the Diet about the Japanese attitude toward international relations.
The critic contended that even as Japan claims it is misunderstood, it
does not try to make itself understood. The dietman smiled ironically.
"That," he said, "is Japanese!"

Perhaps everyone has heard of the mysterious East or the inscrutable
Orient. It may be assumed that the Japanese are inscrutable, for
example, because Oriental cultures are inherently difficult for outsi-
ders to understand. Less frequently suspected is the originally deliberate and later subconscious use of bafflement and mystification, as
part of the ancient art of war.

All sorts of Western attempts to take advantage of Japanese resources, from their economic power to their Zen Buddhism, have been
thwarted or distorted by bafflement and mystification, in cases where
the ulterior logic and method of bafflement and mystification are
unknown. The impression of mystery may appear to veil a secret, but
the main secret may turn out to be that mystery itself is a weapon, an
art of war.

The veil of mystery is just one of the arts of war that permeate
Japanese political, cultural, and social life. For those trying to understand the Japanese mind and civilization—and that may include

anyone involved in the modern world—there is no practical way to overlook the military rule and martial culture that have dominated Japan for many centuries, virtually up to the present day. So steeped in the way of the warrior has Japanese civilization been that some of the manners and mentality of this outlook remain embedded in the deepest strata of the individual and collective unconscious of that nation.

The sword is one of the three basic symbols of Shintō, the ancient Japanese religion, and so of the imperial heritage, which emerged after centuries of racial and tribal wars in ancient Japan. The sword became the soul of the samurai, who gradually extended their control from the frontiers and provinces to become the dominant power in Japan for nearly eight hundred years.

Even in the social and cultural spheres, Japan today still retains indelible impressions of the samurai Bushidō, the way of the warrior. This is true not only in education and the fine arts, but also in characteristic attitudes and conduct marking the course of political, professional, and personal relations. Well-known attributes such as the reserve and the mystery of formal Japanese behavior, as well as the humility and the hauteur, are deeply rooted in the ancient strategies of the traditional art of war. To understand Japan and the Japanese in depth, therefore, it is essential to understand the culture of strategy crafted by the Japanese art of war.

A MARTIAL HISTORY OF JAPAN

The legend of the imperial house of Japan emerged from two stages of armed conquest. The first stage involved the Japanese domination and destruction of other races of people inhabiting the islands that were to become Japan. The second stage, which was partially concurrent with the first, was marked by the ascendancy of some Japanese clans over others.

As the early Japanese grew in numbers and expanded their territories, they subjugated or annihilated the minority races, and also fought among themselves. There were evidently several waves of migration from North Asia resulting in the rise of the people now known as the Japanese. The earliest migrations from the continent through and from the Korean peninsula long predate history. Chinese and Korean culture and technology supported the development of the early Japanese in prehistoric ages, and renewed waves of migration in historical times stimulated by wars, conquests, and empire building continued to enrich and empower dominant Japanese clans.

By the fourth century of the common era, there were dozens of tribal Japanese nations centered around powerful clans of shamanic leaders, hunters and warriors, artisans, and agriculturalists. As the Japanese nations grew, increasing competition and renewed immigration from the continent led to the rise of a powerful alliance of clans who sought an end to hostilities through the establishment of a unified state on the Chinese model. After subduing direct challenges to the central state, the alliance established its priestly clan as the imperial house and organized hierarchies of tribal nobility to accommodate the traditional leaders of the independent nation states within the structure of the proposed unified rule. The mythology of the ancient tribes was then collected and arranged to reflect the political hierarchy of the clans under the imperial rule.

The new central government was not able to exert absolute authority over all the clans in Japan, however, especially not those in more remote areas. An official document issued more than a century after the founding of the imperial state notes the limited extent of central authority and the persistence of territorial competition and conflict. As a customary part of the training of traditional tribal warrior elites, military power was not monopolized by the imperial government, and powerful clans were able to retain considerable independence.

The gradual separation of a cultural aristocracy from a martial aristocracy advanced in pace after the capital of Japan was established in Heian, the ancient city of Kyoto, at the end of the eighth century. Leading families of powerful clans with extensive land holdings gathered in the capital and patronized the development of a colorful and romantic urban culture. In the meanwhile, frontier warrior families continued to expand territories, while provincial warrior families administered and policed the extensive holdings of the court nobles.

After the other inhabitants of the islands had been vanquished and an imperial state with a central bureaucracy had been established, the Japanese warrior elites retained their importance in society through positions as governors of territories and administrators of lands and serfs held by absentee landlords. They also continued to provide the military underpinning of the entire aristocracy, as well as of the various territories and clans.

Armed conflict reemerged along complex lines after the establishment of the social and cultural hierarchy by the imperial clan and its powerful allies. Clan warfare was particularly exacerbated by territorial pressures resulting from the practice of polygamy among the upper classes and the social inequalities built into their customary inheritance practices.

Ultimately the imperial family was dominated by the wealthy Fujiwara clan, which provided all the principal wives of the emperors. The imperial family was also divided within itself across generational lines, with retired emperors often exercising more power from their Buddhist retreats than enthroned emperors did from their courts. Through their extensive connections with the nobility of all ranks, certain Buddhist monasteries also became powerful landholders, complete with their own estates, serfs, industries, banks, governments, and armed forces.

Internal division of power and the lack of strong central direction fostered competition among regional interests, which intensified through the tenth and eleventh centuries. The warrior elites in the provinces gradually increased their demands upon the revenue of the land, wresting more of the power and wealth from the hands of the court aristocrats holding legal title to the land. This political movement also encouraged the warriors to compete among themselves.

By 1100, most of Japan outside of the immediate Heian/Kyoto area was under local military control, and the twelfth century saw virtually constant civil war. In 1185 the most powerful of the warrior clans established a centralized military government, the first of three such regimes to dominate Japanese society, politics, and culture for centuries to come.

The strong military presence marking internal Japanese history has imprinted certain elements of the warrior ethos onto important areas of Japanese thought and society, well beyond the context of the original art of war. For hundreds of years the samurai not only were masters of the political fate of the nation, but were considered the leaders of the popular conscience. The morale and spirit of the warrior was as important to their influence on society as was their material power.

For a few centuries after the importation of T'ang-dynasty Chinese culture to bolster their own national ambitions, the Japanese imperial house and the noble families of its court had maintained extensive land holdings throughout Japan while living a life of luxury in the imperial capital and its environs. The upper-class warriors who administered and policed the estates of the aristocrats gradually increased their own demands for compensation for services rendered, and over the centuries massive blocks of land and land rights came under the control of the samurai. By the end of the twelfth century, a central domestic office of Shōgun, or Generalissimo, was officially recognized and a military paragovernment was established with its own capital in eastern Japan.

During the thirteenth century, the new samurai leaders of Japan again looked to China for inspiration. Now Zen Buddhism and Neo-Confucianism, by this time well established in China as dominant ways of thinking, drew the attention of the Japanese. Both central and local military authorities patronized Zen masters from China, including Japanese pilgrims who had studied Zen in China and Chinese immigrants who were fleeing the invading Mongol conquerors. This patronage ushered in a new epoch in Japanese civilization, in which the warriors superseded the old aristocracy in both political and cultural leadership. Over the following centuries, certain aspects of

Zen and Neo-Confucianism were espoused by the samurai, influencing the development of Bushidō and Japanese ethics.

Near the end of the thirteenth century, the Mongol rulers of China launched two attempts to invade Japan. Momentarily forgetting persistent rivalries among their own military baronies, Japanese warriors fought off one invasion fleet. The other fleet was destroyed by storm winds, said to be a *kamikaze,* or "divine wind," believed to protect the sacred land of Japan. These events left a deep impression on the minds of the samurai, but they also disrupted the military order. As in ancient tribal Japan, in feudal Japan the traditional reward for victory in war was the land conquered; but the defeat of the Mongols did not produce any new territory with which to reward the deeds of the Japanese warriors.

The resulting disgruntlement exacerbated the frictions inherent in the military feudal system, ultimately resulting in the toppling of the reigning dynasty of Shōguns in the fourteenth century. It was replaced by a new Shogunate, established in the imperial capital of Kyoto by another samurai clan and its allies. Never as politically or militarily powerful as the first Shogunate had been in its heyday, the new Kyoto Shogunate went further than its predecessors in patronage of Zen Buddhism and the arts associated with Zen. At the urging of one of the leading Zen masters, the Kyoto Shōgun also renewed contacts with China.

The political fragmentation of the era, however, continued to breed conflict among the baronies. The weaknesses of the feudal lords and the ambitions of the vassals fueled generations of warfare among the various ranks of samurai. The last third of the fifteenth century and most of the sixteenth century saw virtually continuous civil war. Japanese historians describe the life of warriors in those times with the phrase *ge koku jō,* "Those below overcome those above," as long established houses and alliances of warrior chieftains were attacked and overthrown by hungrier samurai from the lower ranks of the military classes.

In spite of the turbulence of this period, known as the era of the Warring States, foreign trade continued according to the enterprise of the various baronies able to participate. In the course of prolonged warfare and military rule, the Japanese had developed what was considered the best swordcraft in Asia and exported enormous quantities of fine steel blades to Ming-dynasty China, itself embroiled in civil war. Japanese freebooters and pirates (*wakō*) were infamous along the coast of China and Southeast Asia, and Japanese colonies were established in the countries along the major trade routes there.

It was near the end of the era of Warring States that Europeans first came to Japan, when both they and the Japanese were at new thresholds in their histories. The powerful warlord Oda Nobunaga soon saw the political and military advantages in welcoming Christianity and Western technology. Waging relentless wars against his rivals, including the wealthy and powerful Tendai, Nichiren, and Shinshū Buddhist sects, Oda reunified nearly all of politically fragmented Japan in the sixteenth century.

After Oda was assassinated by an associate, his former ally Toyotomi Hideyoshi took over Oda's territories and attempted to expand his own control even further. Now somewhat in command of Western weaponry, Hideyoshi distanced himself from the Europeans and began his own imperial ventures. After having consolidated his power in Japan to a degree he deemed sufficient for his purposes, Hideyoshi tried to take Korea and the Philippines. He was completely unsuccessful in these adventures, and his military-political successor Tokugawa Ieyasu ultimately rejected colonialism along with the rest of Western culture, virtually excluding the whole range of Western religious, social, technological, political, and economic ideas and practices.

The isolationist policy initiated by Tokugawa Ieyasu was to last for two and a half centuries, with profound implications for Japan's development on every level from its internal social structure to its international relations. Centuries of free intercourse with the West from the sixteenth century onward would undoubtedly have resulted in not only a different Japan, but a different East Asia. In the context of martial history, had Hideyoshi actively collaborated with European colonialists or recruited European mercenaries, that would have boosted the power of his forays into greater Asia. The main thing that had prevented Japan from becoming a major colonial power in Asia over the two centuries preceding Europe's arrival seems to have been its own internal disunity.

A Japan allied with one or more European powers at the time of its reunification under Oda Nobunaga, Toyotomi Hideyoshi, and Ieyasu four centuries ago would have been able to interact with Asia (and Europe) on terms very different from those of an isolated and technologically backward nation. This in turn would have affected the development of the Muscovite empire in the fifteenth and sixteenth centuries, changing the face of Eurasia.

Japan's retreat into isolationism in the early seventeenth century does not seem to have been motivated simply by insularity, lack of foresight, or the failure of adventures in greater Asia. The Japanese were not sure they could contain the aggressiveness of the Western powers, who were believed to also want Japanese territory and wealth. In its view, the Japanese government seems to have been facing the possibility of direct conflict with the West, and also the possibility of having Western powers fighting for spoils among themselves on Japanese territory.

From a strategic point of view, the Japanese warriors might have tried to safeguard Japan by keeping European allies preoccupied in China and the rest of Asia, but the Western powers seemed intent on reaching everywhere and must have appeared uncontainable to Tokugawa Ieyasu.

Japan finally came out of isolation after two hundred and fifty years of introversion, at the adamant insistence of the Americans, who wanted to trade and seemed prepared to shoot their way in if necessary. After a brief honeymoon with Western civilization, a time of misery for some Japanese and of opportunity for others as the social structure realigned itself to a new environment, the military reasserted control and began to imitate Western imperialism again, just as Hideyoshi had done three centuries earlier.

In 1894–1895, Japan fought a war against China, usurping Taiwan, the Pescadores, and the Liaodong peninsula of Manchuria. This raised some eyebrows, and a consensus of Western powers forced Japan to give back the Liaodong concession. Decades later, in the years before the beginning of World War II, Japanese political writers and speakers were still fuming about this insult. They felt that Japan was arbitrarily being excluded from the modern way of life that the Westerners themselves had urged upon them, a way of life which at that time evidently included, on the level of international politics, the race for power over old Asia.

In 1902, Japan formed an alliance with Great Britain, which enhanced its prestige in the West. This prestige increased dramatically when Japan fought and defeated Russia at war in 1904–1905. Western Europe had been concerned about Russia for some time, as competitors for influence and concessions in Central, South, and West Asia, from Turkey and Armenia to Afghanistan, India, and Tibet.

Although pleased to see Russia take a trouncing, the West could not help wondering whether Japan might not be an even more redoubtable rival if its military capabilities continued to develop at such a rapid pace. The American president Theodore Roosevelt stepped in to negotiate a speedy end to the Russo-Japanese War, and Japan was now recognized as a world power. By 1910, Japan had even been able to annex Korea.

In 1914, Japan officially declared war on Germany and invaded a German leasehold in northeastern China. The following year Japan presented a list of twenty-one demands to the Chinese government, providing that Japan take over Germany's leasehold; that Manchuria and Mongolia be reserved for Japanese colonization and exploitation of resources; that the principal coal mines in China be placed under Japanese control; that no more territory be ceded to other world powers; and that Japan direct China's military, commercial, and financial affairs.

The boldness of these demands is in itself a telling statement of the conditions of those times. The other world powers thwarted Japan's attempt to control China's policy, but China accepted the rest of the Japanese demands. Japan further reinforced its claims in 1917 and extracted a second agreement in 1918. Japan was also awarded the German possessions in northeastern China at the conclusion of World War I, through a secret agreement with the Allies.

After the war, Japanese expansionism turned for a time from military to economic and diplomatic channels. In 1922 Japanese occupation troops were withdrawn from Siberia, where they had been since 1918. In 1923, an enormously destructive earthquake in the capital area wrought havoc on the economy, already seriously weakened by the diversion of easy money from domestic production into foreign imports. The growth of city life around this early burst of consumerism was further exaggerated by the influx of massive numbers of disenfranchised peasants no longer able to pay exorbitant land rents.

The panic of 1929 and the ensuing Great Depression came down on an unstable Japan with devastating force. Cities teemed with unemployed refugees from rural poverty, while the minds of the people were torn by the rift between their traditional frugal ideals and the emphasis on consumption and competition inherent in the influence of Westernization; now certain elements of Japanese political and military thought turned again to expansionism, nationalism, and disciplinarianism.

Expansionism was envisioned as a means of releasing social and economic pressures caused by the rising numbers of unemployed Japanese. Nationalism was seen as a remedy for addictive fascination with things Western, something that had already proved to cause economic problems within the framework of the existing system. An intensified, pseudo-Shintoistic form of nationalism was also used as a justification for Japanese colonial expansion. Disciplinarianism, basically a civil form of militarism sometimes disguised as Zen or Zen martial arts, served as a method of countering the influence of Western democratic libertinism, which was also perceived by reactionary thinkers as a direct threat to the social and economic structure of Japanese society.

In 1931, a desperate Japanese military faction provoked an incident in Manchuria, and Japan quickly occupied that territory as a "response" to the incident. Splitting Manchuria off from China, Japan set up the puppet state Manchukuo. This became a major outpost in Japan's long-term vision of an Asia united under Japanese leadership. Continuing its penetration of northern China through the mid-1930s, Japan turned into a police state at home and an aggressive colonial power abroad.

Finally, cornered by British and American attempts to restrict its acquisition of essential industrial materials for the war effort, Japan proceeded to make the fatal blunder of taking on all its adversaries at once. This same misstep, directly contrary to the classical principles of the art of war, also proved fatal to Japan's ally Germany, which at that time had the most advanced armaments in the world and might have been able to devour the bulk of Europe had it not invaded the Soviet Union so hastily.

After its unconditional surrender to the Allies in 1945, Japan was induced to turn over the results of its grisly Manchurian experiments in modern chemical and germ warfare, and forced to renounce war forever by constitutional decree. At the same time, the emperor of Japan was made to deny his divinity, and the structure of state Shinto was dismantled. In spite of these developments, however, Japan retained a martial force and rebuilt its armament-related industrial capabilities during the Korean War through the patronage of its former enemies.

Even though the Japanese empire was thus dismembered and the threat of Japanese imperialism seemed to have been eliminated by the crushing defeat of 1945, the racial feelings that underlay the fanaticism of Japanese militarism were by no means obliterated. As late as 1960, a book purporting to be about Zen and Shintō was saying that Japan has a divine mission to lead the world; and the Japanese popular press of the 1980s has from time to time revived controversy over whether or not Japan actually surrendered, and whether or not the emperor actually renounced his divinity.

At present, Japan is rapidly approaching global superiority in technology with military applications. Assuming for some reason that Japan will forever identify its own interests with that of its present allies, in recent years the United States has stepped up its pressure on Japan to mitigate the power of its economy by investing more heavily in armaments. Considering the ill will toward the United States that this and related pressures are fostering in the Japanese consciousness, the prudence of this policy is in doubt today when the United States may be in danger of becoming dependent on Japanese technology even in its own national defense.

Other Asian nations, which bore the brunt of Japanese militarism earlier in this century, are certainly conscious of the dangers of military revival in Japan and have expressed their alarm at signs of Japanese ultranationalism perceived in diplomatic, economic, educational, and military spheres of activity. In this respect the Western nations, the United States in particular, are seen as either too arrogant or too naive to fully realize that the attempt to resolve economic problems by expanding the armament industry carries with it dangers that history has already shown to be ultimately beyond the control of diplomacy alone.

ZEN IN JAPANESE HISTORY

Politics and religion have been intimately connected throughout most of Japanese history. Zen is one of several schools of Japanese Buddhism to arise in concert with the decline of the court aristocracy and the establishment of a centralized power structure by the military elite. It is the only one of these schools to have been freshly imported from China, lending it even greater prestige in the eyes of its samurai adherents.

Zen was patronized by the early Shōguns partly as a ploy to foster a sort of cultural revolution to enhance the prestige and legitimacy of warriors as secular leaders. Therefore, it has come to be associated with the military class, and even called the religion of the samurai.

Zen was not the only sect of Buddhism that attracted adherents from among the warriors, however, and professional warriors were by no means any more successful in mastering Zen than were members of any other class. There remain, nevertheless, seemingly indelible traces of militaristic influence on Japanese Zen as well as Zen influence on the Japanese military. Eventually it became difficult to separate the two directions of influence, even as both affected the political and cultural life of the nation.

The newly introduced Chinese Zen brought Neo-Confucianism into Japan along with its own special teachings. A combination of ancient Confucian social idealism and Buddhist mysticism, Neo-Confucianism was used by the early Zen masters in their attempt to instill humanistic values in the minds of the new warrior elite.

At first Zen also produced a vigorous inspiration toward pure spirituality, and the movement of warriors to bend Zen to their own ends does not seem to have taken over until several generations later. From the time of the second Shogunate, however, there is a clear distinction to be made between the Zen of spirit and the Zen of power. The gap between politicized church Zen and spiritual Zen grew throughout the Middle Ages, until there was almost nothing left of the latter by the time of the founding of the third Shogunate in the early seventeenth century.

Zen and the other new schools of Japanese Buddhism arising around the late twelfth and early thirteenth centuries were facilitated by the decline of the court aristocracy that had patronized the established churches and by the deterioration of the upper-class Buddhist priesthood. The early Zen masters were learned monks of the classical schools who had become revolted by the materialism and politicization of church Buddhism and who had been unable to find practical solutions within the current curricula.

Some of these monks went to China in search of answers, and found Chan (Zen), a form of Buddhism unlike what was generally known in Japan at that time. Although Chan had been flourishing centuries earlier when groups of Japanese pilgrims went to China in search of knowledge for the development of Japanese civilization, at that time almost all of the Chan schools went unnoticed by the pilgrims. By the thirteenth century, however, Chan Buddhism had penetrated the fabric of Chinese civilization so deeply and its teachers and schools had attained such prestige over hundreds of years of continuous work, that it was by then the preeminent form of Buddhism in China.

Chinese Chan Buddhism was, however, already considered by its own leading masters to be in a moribund state when the Japanese began to import it in earnest. Already six hundred years old, Chan Buddhism suffered from the ordinary ailments of institutionalization that arise from the arousal of proprietary sentiments in regard to a religion or an organization. Chan also suffered from a parallel involution in its method, with increasing intricacy and formalization vitiating its efficiency.

The early Japanese Zen pilgrims were already learned in classical Buddhist theory and had personally witnessed institutional decadence in even more extreme forms in their own churches. These factors undoubtedly helped them in their Zen studies in China, and most of them returned to Japan within five or six years. Since China was itself in a state of ferment, the Japanese pilgrims were generally not able to travel extensively and therefore did not meet many of the Chinese Zen masters. On the other hand, the Japanese Zen movement was also fertilized by Chinese monks seeking political refuge from the regime of the Mongol Yuan dynasty.

According to historians, as many as twenty-seven or more schools of Zen were set up in medieval Japan, most of which were affiliated with the sect of Rinzai (Chinese Lin-chi or Linji). Zen students were not bound to any school and commonly studied in more than one of them. This diluted their identities as separate schools, and only a few of the original Zen lineages continued to exist for more than three or four generations after being imported into Japan.

The second Shogunate, which replaced the first one in the fourteenth century, patronized Zen Buddhism in the Kyoto area, using its facilities not only for religious purposes but as a foundation of learning and culture in general. Zen arts of scholarship, poetry, painting, ritual, and environmental design were developed and elaborated throughout this period. The Kyoto Shogunate also reopened communications with China at the suggestion of the leading Zen master of its early days.

Interest in Chinese culture during this period reached the point where groups of as many as fifty Japanese Zen pilgrims were going on tours of Chinese monasteries. The manifest influence of Zen on Japanese culture had reached its zenith. The government established a twin hierarchy of elite Zen monasteries headed by establishments around the seats of the first and second Shogunates in Kamakura and Kyoto. The liberal education of upper-class samurai was entrusted largely to the learned Zen monks of the capital.

These schools are especially famous for their poetry, art, and secular scholarship, but the elite monastic society in the service of the upper classes came to be considered decadent and spiritually bankrupt in terms of the original Zen enlightenment. Followers of spiritual Zen tended to avoid the prestigious monasteries, preferring to look for unobtrusive masters in the provinces. In later generations, practitioners of Zen had little use for the poetry of the elite Zen institutions known as the Gozan, or "Five Mountains." The tradition of secular Five Mountain poetry and scholarship was continued by Neo-Confucian specialists who eventually broke away from Zen churches, while the tradition of Zen poetry for practical rather than ornamental use was renewed in a later Zen revival movement.

Because of the corruption in its institutions, by the end of the fifteenth century Zen was virtually extinct spiritually, if not socially and politically. An exceptional Zen monk of the fifteenth century, the beloved folk figure Ikkyū, wrote that the Zen schools had all lost their transmission and were names without realities. Considered one of the very greatest Japanese Zen masters in history, Ikkyū was an incisive critic with an irrepressible sense of humor. His vernacular writings forged a unique link with popular culture, and he was eventually turned into a folkloric figure, the subject of countless tales of wit and wisdom.

Ikkyū is famous for carrying around a wooden sword, saying that the Zen of the time did not even have the "killing sword" of penetrating insight, let alone the "life-giving sword" of objective compassion. He is also said to have destroyed his *inka shōmei,* a traditional testament of approval given him by his Zen teacher. According to one story, Ikkyū destroyed such a document twice, saying that it had lost its meaning in the contemporary milieu, with the disappearance of Zen enlightenment and the proliferation of corrupt Zen priests. He also wrote that people had formerly gone to monasteries to seek enightenment, but now they were leaving monasteries to seek enlightenment.

It is difficult to find many records of the works of authentic Zen masters in the sixteenth century; only a few fragments and anecdotes remain of them. Intellectual Zen monks in the capital were involved in art, literature, education, and politics, but Zen practice had become so formalized that few of them attained enlightenment. Except for the activities of a relatively small number of practitioners outside the major urban establishments, Zen Buddhism had largely become a cultural movement.

The state of Zen Buddhism changed radically in the seventeenth century, with the rejection of the cultural and intellectual Zen of the Middle Ages and the establishment of vigorous new schools of Zen teaching. Civil wars ended and the Tokugawa Peace was established throughout Japan, making it easier for students to go on pilgrimage to recollect the scattered lore of medieval Zen practice. There was also a movement to revive study of the Chinese Chan classics, in parallel with a movement to abstract the essence of Zen practice for popular use. In many cases the same Zen masters were active in both movements. These Zen masters, most of whom still avoided the long-corrupted elite monastic establishments, succeeded in bringing about a great revival in Zen Buddhism.

This revival reached its apogee around the middle of the eighteenth century, and stagnated thereafter. One obstacle to the further development of Zen was government policy, under which a number of measures were instituted to rigorously circumscribe the activities and influence of Buddhism. All monasteries, nunneries, and temples, even in the most remote provinces, were incorporated into a hierarchy under the authority of one of the elite central monasteries, which were in turn under the authority of the military government.

Provincial temples were also incorporated directly into the government machinery, serving as the equivalent of today's city halls and registry offices. Many local temples also ran primary schools, but the curriculum was limited to the version of Neo-Confucianism sanctioned by the government. Lay people were forbidden to teach Buddhism, even if they were recognized as competent by Zen authorities themselves. Each sect of Buddhism was required to submit a list of doctrines, and these were then declared dogma by the state; innovation was now officially forbidden.

Buddhism had always been considered something of a threat to the state when it was not part of the state's own mechanism of authority. The Tokugawa attempt to prematurely fossilize Buddhism and reduce its power was initiated in the seventeenth century, with the resurgence of Zen itself. This external threat to the spiritual life of Zen was then compounded in the eighteenth century by attachment to the forms of religion.

According to Zen technical literature, characteristic symptoms of attachment to forms include fascination with secondary phenomena and an inability to gain access to the source of creativity. This is viewed as a habit of mind that is ordinarily enacted on both individual and collective levels of human history and must be newly transcended in every generation. Involution set in again as Zen became intricate, arcane, and forced, in repeated attempts to wring generation after generation of inspiration out of limited systems and doctrines. The official curriculum became a caricature of the originally flexible Zen teachings that had initiated the seventeenth-century revival.

In the middle of the nineteenth century, with the replacement of the third Shogunate by direct imperial rule and the end of late feudal Japan's radical isolationism, Zen Buddhism was subjected to new pressures. From within Japan, Buddhism was attacked as a foreign religion by the establishment of state Shintō under the leadership of the emperor. This antiforeign and anti-Buddhist trend was ideologically backed by extremists of a xenophobic academic movement called Patriotic Studies (Kokugaku), which had arisen in the previous century and now commanded great prestige. Many Buddhist temples were confiscated and converted to Shintō shrines.

From abroad, Buddhism was threatened by aggressive Christian

missions attempting to link the Western technical kn
avidly sought by the Japanese with Christianity as und
West. Since part of the Christian missionary method v
and rebuke the local religions it hoped to supplant,
Western scholarship on Buddhism began from this
shaped by its purpose.

Japanese Buddhists reacted to European polemics in different ways.
Some of them plunged more deeply into Buddhist scriptures and
classics to defend their faith against Western slander. Others became
fanatical yogis, disciplinarians, or martial artists. Yet others imitated
the methods of Western scholastics and tried to use them to analyze
their own classics and histories, becoming professional academics and
intellectuals in conformity with European models.

Traces of all of these trends still exist in Japan today, but the yogic,
disciplinarian, and martialized forms of Zen and Buddhism tend to
attract more general interest than either traditional or Westernized
academics. After the fall of the last Shogunate and the end of state
patronage of Buddhism, increasing attention was given to winning
popular enthusiasm and support. One of the outstanding pioneers of
this movement was an unusual Zen monk named Nantembō (1839–
1925), who had grown up in feudal Japan and later attracted many
followers among the aristocracy and the military elite.

Nantembō rocked the Rinzai Zen world with his blasting attacks
on its hereditary priesthood and campaigned for a universal qualifying
system for Rinzai Zen masters. Failing to persuade the authorities to
institute such a system, Nantembō eventually gave up hope of reform-
ing monastic Zen. Considering established monastic Zen politically
and morally corrupt, he devoted his time to developing lay Zen. He
generated a wave of enthusiasm by introducing a special technique
for rapid attainment of concentration and ecstasy. His intensive
meditation retreats became popular among the social elite, whose
families were traditionally patrons of Rinzai Zen or were involved in
the classical arts anciently associated with Rinzai Zen.

Although only a few disciples of this Zen master learned his
complete teaching, he had thousands of lay followers, and his influence
was widely diffused through extensive correspondence, personal in-
terviews, and Zen revival meetings in which people would gather for
intensive concentration exercises punctuated by rough-and-tumble
encounters with the master. Nantembō himself claimed that six
hundred people had attained experience of an elementary stage of

_en under his guidance, including some of the most prominent people in civil and military society.

Since Namtembō's intensive technique as employed in his crash programs was therefore spread without the context of the whole teaching, the dangers inherent in such a method often went unchecked among Zen enthusiasts of subsequent generations. The militant ferocity of the style of training used by Nantembō and other old Zen monks brought up in feudal times was absorbed not only by the military and police forces through the schools of hard martial arts they pursued, but also by the civilian world throught the *jigoku* ("hell") methods used to train students and corporate employees.

Nantembō's methods spread further through one of his erstwhile disciples, a layman whom he acknowledged to have passed through the whole system but who eventually left the master, saying he "had no eyes." Although this expression normally refers to blindness or ignorance, it can have several meanings. Sometimes it refers to naive ignorance in the sense of lack of awareness. It can also be used to refer to cultivated ignorance, such as comes about through fixation on totems.

The term is also a classic description of a kind of "Zen illness" caused by overindulgence in excessive concentration on meditation of the type that stops the mind. On the most refined level, the expression means that the Zen master in question is absorbed in nirvana. In this last connection it is interesting to note that Nantembō was one of the rare latter-day Zen masters to have his funeral held before he died, an ancient ceremony performed for certain warriors, priests, and human sacrifices.

The meaning of the graduate disciple leaving Nantembō and going to another teacher depends on the intention of the statement that Namtembō had no eyes. However this matter may be interpreted, it is clear that the former disciple brought at least part of the intensive technique of Nantembō to his new school, through which it spread even further, particularly among lay Zen practitioners.

Some Zennists have also used this kind of method in attempts to popularize Zen in the West, on the premise that the rapidity and drama of its initial effects would be able to interest and inspire Westerners as yet unaccustomed to more subtle impressions. Certain imitations of this sort of technique have also developed elsewhere in modern Western culture through interaction with a dilute yet discernible input from Japanese Zen culture.

The blinding side effects of overestimating and overusing hyperin-
tensive methods showed up again in later generations and remain
among the issues faced by modern Zen schools and the training
systems of the movements they have influenced. Parallel and derivative
techniques have already appeared in the West, sponsored by both
Japanese and Western organizations and employed in both religious
and secular contexts. These relics of feudalistic martial styles of Zen
are so intimately connected with the *jigoku* "hell" style of Japanese
soldier-citizen training that their background in Bushidō stands out
for objective examination in any pragmatic study of the interface
between Japanese and Western cultures, whether in the realm of
religion, education, or industry.

BUSHIDŌ AND MARTIAL ARTS

In his famous *Book of Five Spheres,* the swordsman Miyamoto Musashi introduces the subject of the art of war as one among the various traditional Ways of Japanese culture, to be studied and practiced by political leaders as well as by professional warriors.

> The arts of warfare are the science of military experts. Leaders in particular practice these arts, and soldiers should also know this science. In the present day there are no warriors with accurate understanding of the science of martial arts.

Shortly before Musashi's birth, Japan had been more or less reunified after a century of civil wars. His era was still highly militarized, and marked by armed conflict at home and abroad. He died shortly after the final destruction of opposition to the new Shogunate established during his lifetime. Writing his classic of strategy near the end of his life, Musashi claims that no warriors of his day really understood the martial arts; it is not clear whether he regarded this lapse of tradition to be rooted in the conditions of war or the conditions of peace.

It is evident, nevertheless, that Musashi regarded the way of the warrior as a special calling. As with any other Way, mastery depended in great measure on the affinity of the practitioner with the path. Musashi compares the art of war with other arts as a specialization demanding its own characteristic inclination.

> People practice the ways to which they are inclined, developing individual preferences. Buddhism is a way of helping people, Confucianism is a way of civilization, healing is a way of curing illnesses. Poets teach the way of poetry, others take to the ways of fortune telling, archery, and various other arts and crafts. Few people like the art of war.

Musashi's assertion that few people like the martial arts contrasts sharply with their modern popularity, both in Asia and in the West.

In Musashi's time, however, the way of the warrior was not a hobby but a total lifestyle. Such a life involved rigors and perils that were soon to disappear, even from the world of the Japanese samurai.

One characteristic Musashi's way had in common with classical Chinese philosophical concepts of warriorhood was his emphasis on a balanced combination of practical learning in both cultural and martial arts: "First of all," he wrote, "the way of warriors means familiarity with both cultural and martial arts." In ancient China, when wars were still fought exclusively by men of the aristocratic houses, the single word *shi*, or "knight," meant both scholar and warrior. The training of this class of men was considered to be one of the most important tasks of the culture.

In later times, scholars were still schooled in martial arts, while warriors were also taught cultural arts. This practice was taken up by the upper-class samurai in Japan, where the identification of the civil and military elites was more complete and longer lasting than in China. While he followed the tradition of the cultured warrior in both theory and practice, however, because of his background Musashi inevitably laid greater stress on martial arts.

> Even if they are clumsy at this, individual warriors should strengthen their own martial arts as much as practical under the circumstances. . . . In China and Japan, practitioners of this science have been legendary as masters of martial arts. Warriors should not fail to learn this science.

One of the characteristics of the warrior's way that seems to distinguish it from the way of culture is the ever-presence of death. It is commonly said that one reason warriors liked Zen Buddhism was because it taught them to face death with equanimity. Musashi, himself deeply interested in Zen, rejects this reasoning.

> People usually assume that all warriors think about is getting used to the imminent possibility of death. As far as the process of death is concerned, warriors are not the only ones who die. All classes of people know their duty, are ashamed to neglect it, and realize that death is inevitable. There is no difference among social groups in this respect.

From the point of view of cultural transmission, or transcultural communication, it is noteworthy that this passage from Musashi's *Book of Five Spheres* has been rendered differently by some translators, in such a way as to draw a distinction between the way of the warrior and the ways of other walks of life. Considering the central importance of death in both Buddhism and Bushidō, this is worth examination.

Two translators construe Musashi as saying that people other than warriors only resign themselves to death when duty or disgrace commands them to do so. Grammatically, this is within the realm of possibility, but Musashi does not overtly say this—something he could easily have done with but a single particle. One translator even replaces the last line with its opposite, saying that the way of warriors and the ways of the other walks of life are completely different. These readings seem to be strongly influenced by the very preconceptions Musashi is dismissing. This phenomenon is also common in translations of certain Zen writings.

In the literal meaning of the original, Musashi's statement specifically includes monks and nuns, women, farmers, and "even those below them," which would mean artisans, merchants, outcastes, and untouchables. In Musashi's own lifetime the ancient Japanese class system underwent its most extreme phase of ossification, hardened by government fiat into a caste system. Most people were simply born into a way of life that they had no choice but to accept; that became their duty and their reason for being. Death was the only alternative.

But there were different grades of death in Musashi's world. There was social death, and there was physical death. Some people chose physical death when they experienced social death, and this choice was always honored if properly executed. On the other hand, people who had failed in their own walks of life could possibly run away and join despised professions frequently pursued by untouchables, becoming tinkers, peddlers, undertakers, shoemakers, and so on. They could also join the world of the outcastes, becoming prostitutes, panders, gamblers, and entertainers. Another possibiity was to become a monk or a nun, although as monks and nuns in those times people still might wind up in one of the untouchable or outcaste demimondes.

The outstanding fact of seventeenth-century Japanese society, however, was that people in all walks of life realized the inevitabilty of death without having to connect that with duty or conscience at all. Ordinary peasants were just as close to death as any warriors, let alone the bureaucratic warriors for whom the martial arts were a pastime. The policy of the Shogunate was to keep people uncertain of their fate, and they did not need Buddhism to remind them of the evanescence of life.

Farmers, who comprised four-fifths of the population at that time, were taxed so intensively that they were constantly dogged by starvation. They were also subject to the threat of *burei-uchi* ("being killed for insolence") whenever they were in the presence of samurai. So whether they were warriors or peasants, it was not that the traditional culture of Buddhism reminded people of death so much as that the real nearness of death provoked interest in Buddhism.

Therefore Musashi denied the usual idea that awareness of imminent death is the prime distinguishing mood of the warrior's way. Instead, he said it is the overriding need to win. Even granting the relatively limited role of competition in Musashi's times, he is perhaps naive in regarding this need to win as particular to warriors, as naive as he deemed others in their opinions. The narrowness of his thinking in this respect, on the other hand, is not his own but a byproduct of the caste system in which he lived.

Reflecting his point of view as a samurai in feudal Japan, Musashi describes the way of the warrior in the following terms:

> The way of carrying out the martial arts of warriors is in all events based on excelling others. Whether in winning an individual duel, or winning a fight with several people, one thinks of serving the interests of one's employer, of serving one's own interests, of becoming well known and socially established. This is all possible by martial arts.

This was already true of other professions in Musashi's time, and it is even more so in the present day. The popularity of writings by Musashi and other warriors today attests to their relevance to other walks of life. Musashi himself amends his view elsewhere in the book. As for the martial arts themselves, the formal stylization and abstraction that characterize them today were already beginning when Musashi wrote his famous treatise, years after the last of the dynastic wars. Because of this, Musashi warns against dilettantism in the warrior's way, stressing the need for ability to apply it. The way must not only be useful in combat, he writes, but in every aspect of life as well.

> There are no doubt people who think that even to be practicing martial arts will not prove useful when a real need arises. As far

as that is concerned, the true way of martial arts is to practice them in such a way that they will be useful at any time, and to teach them in such a way that they will be useful in all things.

In this connection, Musashi laments the commercialization of martial arts, resulting in fragmentation of the science, with impractical elaborations and movements based on showmanship rather than on efficiency in warfare.

In recent times, people who make their living as martial artists are swordmasters only. It is only in latter days that Shintō priests from certain regions travel the provinces teaching people various styles of swordplay that the priests developed and passed on as having been transmitted from the spirits.

The practice of attributing arts and sciences to ancient or even divine precedents is not uncommon in the East. The martial art known as T'ai Chi Ch'uan or Taijiquan ("absolute boxing"), for example, is sometimes said to have been first revealed to its originator by a spirit in a dream. Note here how Musashi associates popular schools of martial arts with Shinto, not Zen Buddhism. He goes on to speak of the "art of the advantage," the abstract core of the art of war.

Since ancient times "the art of the advantage" has been added to traditional arts and crafts, but once we are talking about the art of the advantage, this shouldn't be limited to swordsmanship alone. What is more, swordsmanship itself can hardly be known by considering only how to win by use of the sword.

"The art of the advantage" is a more inclusive term than "martial arts," in that it refers to the science of strategy in general. Here the practical meaning of martial arts deviates somewhat from their function in Zen training, insofar as it is focused on personal advantage rather than on resourcefulness itself. Musashi goes on to speak of the alienation of all the arts from their educational applications through commercialization.

As I see society, people make the arts into commercial products. They even think of themselves as commodities, and also make implements for their commercial value. This attitude is like flowers compared with seeds: the flowers are more numerous than the seeds; there is more decoration than reality.

In martial arts particularly there is a lot of showmanship and commercial popularization. The result of this must be, as someone said, "Amateuristic martial arts are a source of serious wounds."

Musashi therefore insisted on technical expertise in the fundamentals of the warrior's craft, much as would be required in any profession. For warriors this means knowledge of weaponry, but Musashi's admonitions on this point have the power of unlimited metaphor:

> The science of martial arts for warriors requires construction of various weapons and understanding the properties of the weapons. A member of a warrior familly who does not learn to use weapons and understand the specific advantages of each weapon would seem to be somewhat uncultivated.

Extending this general principle further in his simile of the master carpenter, Musashi stresses the wisdom of learning all aspects and all skills of a profession or business. This underlay the ancient institution of apprenticeship, through which people might master a trade in every respect through a natural process of development. The principle has also been applied by the Japanese in the corporate world of the latter half of the twentieth century, and is one of the major factors supporting well-known technical and sociological successes seen in Japanese business and industry. Musashi writes:

> I will use the way of carpentry to talk about the martial arts. The simile of the carpenter refers to the master carpenter who builds houses. Aristocrats, military families, and schools of art and culture are all spoken of in terms of tradition, style, and "house," so since we are using the expression "house" I have used the mastery of carpentry as a symbol.

Use of the image of a master carpenter to represent leadership goes back to ancient Taoist classics, and is particularly marked in the political treatises of *Huainanzi*, one of the major books of philosophical Taoism. Although it was not commonly studied in Japan, Musashi may have come in contact with this book through his association with Zen Buddhism. Taoist scholarship is known to have been one of the many accomplishments of the famous Zen master Takuan, an elder contemporary of Musashi and teacher of the Shōgun and of the master swordsman Yagyū Munenori.

In any case, the organizational ideas Musashi used had become traditional because of the prestige of their source, especially in a cultural milieu under the influence of Zen. In *Book of Five Spheres*, Musashi explains his own craft in the classic metaphor, thus leaving its own symbolic potential unbounded:

> The word for carpenter is written with the characters for "great skill." Since the science of the art of war is a great skill, it is symbolized by the carpenter. If you want to learn the science of the art of war, meditate on this book; let the teacher be the needle and the student be the thread, and practice it always.
>
> As the master carpenter is the overall organizer and director of the journeymen, it is the duty of the master carpenter to understand the system of measurement, keep local measurements accurate, and attend to the measurements of the master carpenter's own establishment.
>
> The master carpenter, knowing how to build all sorts of structures, employs people to erect houses. In this respect the master carpenter is the same as the master warrior.
>
> When sorting out timber for building a house, if logs that look good, logs that are straight and without knots, are used for front pillars; logs with some knots but still straight and strong are used for back pillars; logs that may be somewhat weak but have no knots and look good are used for framing; and logs that may be gnarled and crooked but nevertheless strong are used thoughtfully in consideration of the various members of the house, then the house will last a long time. Even gnarled, crooked, and weak logs can be used for scaffolding, and can be made into firewood later.
>
> As the master carpenter directs the journeymen, he knows their various levels of skill and gives them appropriate tasks. Even the unskilled and the clumsy can be given chores suiting their abilities. If the master carpenter exercises discernment in assignment of jobs, work progresses smoothly. Efficiency and smooth progress, prudence in all matters, knowing the total dynamic, knowing different levels of energy and temperament, instilling confidence, knowing what is not possible—such are the matters on the mind of the master carpenter. This is the way it is with the martial arts.

The Taoist classic *Huainanzi* talks about social equality in terms of full employment according to individual abilities. Under the direction of sages, according to the ancient book of statecraft, "there are no wasted people and no wasted things." This is the art of a master politician as well as the art of a master warrior. Now Musashi turns his attention to the position of the apprentice.

> As journeymen, warriors sharpen their own tools; they make various useful implements and keep them in their carpentry boxes. Following the intructions of the master carpenter, they do all the necessary tasks, making sure the measurements are correct and seeing that all the work is done properly. This is the rule for journeymen.
>
> When they have developed practical knowledge of all the skills of the craft, eventually they may become master carpenters themselves.
>
> An essential habit for carpenters is to have sharp tools and keep them whetted. It is up to the carpenter to use those tools to fashion a whole range of articles. This is the way it is for warriors.

As Musashi himself suggests, this is not only the way things are for warriors, but also the way things are for everyone else in a changing world where skills and fluidity are essential tools of survival. While the outer framework of the warrior's learning is based on the interdependence of many factors, the inner dimension of it is based on the relationship between the learner and the learning. The precise balancing of outer and inner elements was always considered one of the highest skills of mastery, and was an art studied with particular attention by ancient Zen schools.

The swordsman Yagyū Munenori, an older contemporary of Musashi who also took an intense interest in Zen, wrote extensively on the Zen attitude toward learning in his *Book on Family Traditions in the Art of War*, where he based his argument on what he had heard from Zen master Takuan.

> Masters of the arts cannot be called adepts as long as they have not left behind attachments to their various skills.
>
> A mendicant asked an ancient saint, "What is the Way?"
>
> The saint said, *"The normal mind is the Way."*
>
> The principle of this story applies to all arts. This is the stage where sicknesses of the mind are all gone, when you have become

normal in mind and have no sicknesses even while in the midst of sicknesses.

As Yagyū explains later, "sickness" here means fixation or lingering of the attention. This is considered an abnormality or deviation from the Zen ideal in that it results in inhibition of spontaneous responsiveness and free function. Therefore Yagyū extols the level of expertise at which one reaches "normalcy" in the Zen sense of natural, unselfconscious mastery in one's occupation.

> To apply this to worldly matters, suppose you are shooting and you think you're shooting while you're shooting: then the aim of your bow will be inconsistent and unsteady. When you wield a sword, if you are conscious of wielding a sword, your offense will be unstable. When you are writing, if you are conscious of writing, your pen will be unsteady. Even when you play the harp, if you are conscious of playing, the tune will be off.
>
> When an archer forgets consciousness of shooting, and shoots in a normal frame of mind, as if unoccupied, the bow will be steady. When using a sword or riding a horse as well, you don't "wield a sword" or "ride a horse." And you don't "write," you don't "play music." When you do everything in the normal state of mind, as it is when totally unoccupied, then everything goes smoothly and easily.
>
> Whatever you do is your Way. If you are obsessed with it, or think that this alone is of importance to you, then it is not the Way. It is when you have nothing in your chest that you are on the Way. Whatever you do, if you do it with nothing in your chest, it works out easily.

There is a Zen proverb that says, "This is it, but if you fixate on it, then it isn't anymore." This means that immediate reality is itself enlightenment, as Zen teaching so often states, unless the conceptual recognition that "this is it" replaces the direct experience, triggering the mechanism of fixation all over again. Therefore the symbol of the mirror, reflecting spontaneously without subjectivity and without retaining any images, came to be used as a popular simile for the basic Zen mind. Yagyū continues:

> This is like the way everything reflects clearly in a mirror precisely because of the formless clarity of the mirror's reflective-

ness. The heart of those on the Way is like a mirror, empty and clear, being mindless yet not failing to accomplish anything.

This is the "normal mind." Someone who does everything with this normal mind is called an adept.

Whatever you do, if you keep the idea of doing it before you and do it with singleminded concentration, you will be uncoordinated. You'll do it well once, and then, when you think that's fine, now you'll do it badly. Or you may do it well twice, then do it badly again. If you're glad you did it well twice and badly only once, then you'll do it badly again. There is no consistency at all, because of doing it with the thought of doing it well.

When effective work builds up unawares and practice accumulates, thoughts of quickly developing skill quietly disappear, and whatever you do you spontaneously become free from conscious thoughts. At this time you don't even know yourself; when your body, feet, and hands act without you doing anything in your mind, you make no misses, ten times out of ten. Even then, if it gets on your mind at all, you'll miss. When you are not consciously mindful, you'll succeed every time.

However, not being consciously mindful does not mean total mindlessness; it just means a normal mind.

Zen master Takuan explained the paradoxical relationship between training and spontaneity to Yagyū Munenori in terms that the swordsman would later incorporate into his own family tradition of martial arts. The Zen master wrote to the warrior:

> You need to realize that when you practice from the state of the beginner all the way to the stage of immutable wisdom, then you must go back to the status of the beginner again.
>
> Let me explain in terms of your martial arts. As a beginner you know nothing of stance or sword position, so you have nothing in yourself to dwell on mentally. If someone strikes at you, you just fight, without thinking of anything.
>
> Then when you learn various things like stance, how to wield a sword, where to place the attention, and so on, your mind lingers on various points, so you find yourself all tangled up when you try to strike.
>
> But if you practice day after day and month after month, eventually stance and swordplay don't hang on your mind anymore, and you are like a beginner who knows nothing.

This is the sense in which it is said that the beginning and the end are the same, just as one and ten become neighbors when you have counted from one to ten. It is also like the highest and lowest notes of a musical scale becoming neighbors below and above a cycle of the scale.

Just as the highest and lowest notes resemble each other, since buddhas are the highest human development they appear to be like people who know nothing of Buddha or Buddhism, having none of the external trappings that people envision of buddhas.

Therefore the afflictions of unaware lingering in the beginning and the immutable wisdom in the end become one. The cogitating side of your brain will vanish, and you will come to rest in a state where there is no concern.

Completely ignorant people don't show their wits, it seems, because they haven't got any. Highly developed intelligence doesn't show because it has already gone into hiding. It is because of pseudo-erudition that intelligence goes to one's head, a ludicrous sight.

A Taoist proverb says, "A clever merchant hides his goods and pretends to have nothing." Taoist and Zen classics also speak of "softening the light to harmonize with the world." Self-conscious display is considered not only unbecoming but counterproductive. A Sung-dynasty Chinese Zen master said, "Those who have no real virtue within but outwardly rely on flowery cleverness are like leaky boats brightly painted—if you put manikins in them and set them on dry ground they look all right, but once they go into the rivers and lakes, into the wind and waves, are they not in danger?"

The practice of "hiding one's light" so as to appear ordinary to others was carried on deliberately by ancient Buddhist and Taoist mystics after they had attained enlightenment, believing that they could thereby reach higher levels of refinement than if they allowed themselves to be admired for their knowledge. This was a higher form of modesty than that prescribed for students, for whom the compulsion to show off was considered fatally destructive to their chances for enlightenment. Fushan, one of the great Chinese Zen masters, said, "Those who flash their learning and run off at the mouth without having ever learned to actually attain the Way, using eloquence and sharpness of tongue to gain victories, are like outhouses painted vermilion. The vermilion only increases the odor."

In his own book of family traditions, Yagyū both concentrates and expands upon the teaching of Zen master Takuan.

It becomes easier to do everything when you come to have nothing on your mind. For this reason, study of all the Zen arts is for the purpose of clearing away what is on your mind. In the beginning you don't know anything; you hardly even have any questions on your mind. Then when you enter into study, there is something on your mind, and you are blocked by it. This makes everything difficult to do.

When what you have studied leaves your mind entirely, and practice also disappears, then when you perform whatever art you are engaged in, you accomplish the techniques easily, without being concerned over what you have practiced, and yet without deviating from what you have practiced. This is spontaneously conforming without being aware that you are doing so.

In virtually all domains of traditional Japanese arts, it was customary to begin with strict adherence to standard forms and rites. This was supposed to induce the student to get the "feel" of the art intuitively, without stopping to rationalize and project subjective ideas onto the action itself. The purpose of this rigid discipline, however, was not to automatize the learner but to provide a dependable framework of support for an extra faculty of perception that could be exercised once conscious attention to the formal foundation was no longer necessary.

The ultimate goal of freedom and spontaneity was thus not pursued arbitrarily, but in accord with a gradual process that had already been tested. Adepts who had passed beyond formal systems were known to discover techniques and movements naturally, without having learned them from a teacher.

Zen master Takuan summed up his discussion of independent spontaneity and factual practice in terms of principle and action.

There is the practice of principle and the practice of action. Principle is as mentioned before: when you have arrived at mastery, you don't struggle with anything. It is all in the way you give up minding at all.

However, if you don't do practice of action, you will only have principle in mind and won't be able to do anything about it.

In Buddhist terminology, "principle" is often used synonymously with "emptiness" or "noumenon," which means subjective mental freedom in Zen psychology. The need to practice "action" refers to the externalization of inner freedom, a more advanced level of Zen mastery. Principle also means theory, which is ineffective without applicable practice.

The warrior Musashi also followed the Zen teaching on clarity and fluidity of mind as the basis of the art of learning itself, as applicable to the martial arts and the way of the warrior as to any other art or way. In the "Water Scroll" of Musashi's *Book of Five Spheres*, the warrior writes in a vein similar to that of Yagyū and Takuan, with more technical elaboration.

> According to the science of martial arts, the state of mind should remain the same as normal. Center your mind so that there is no imbalance, no difference between your ordinary mind and your mind when practicing martial arts. Let your mind be broad and direct, neither tense nor lax. Calmly relax your mind, and savor this moment of ease thoroughly, so that the relaxation does not stop its relaxation even for an instant.
>
> Even when you are still, your mind is not still; even when hurried, your mind is not hurried. The mind is not dragged by the body, the body is not dragged by the mind. Pay attention to the mind, not the body. Let there be neither insufficiency nor excess in your mind. Even if superficially weakhearted, be inwardly stronghearted, and don't let others see into your mind.
>
> Let your inner mind be unclouded and open, placing your intellect on a broad plane. It is essential to polish the intellect and mind diligently. Once you have sharpened your intellect to the point where you can see whatever is reasonable and what is not, where you can tell whatever is good or bad, and when you are experienced in various fields and are incapable of being fooled at all by people of the world, then your mind becomes imbued with the knowledge of the art of war.
>
> There is something special about knowledge of the art of war: it is imperative to master the principles of the art of war and to learn to be unmoved in mind even in the heat of battle.

As the testaments of Yagyū and Musashi illustrate, warriors followed the Zen teaching on emptying the mind for several purposes: one was to learn the secret of learning itself; another was to learn to act with spontaneous efficiency, free from doubt, hesitation, and fear, in whatever circumstances they might find themselves; they wanted to see realities independently, without extraneous influences; and they wanted to learn to see things before they happened, to make themselves invulnerable to enemies and become masters of their own fate.

This last function of the Zen technique depends on sharpening discernment of the fine web of subtle causal relations by removing the veil of mental preoccupations. Zen teachers use it for predicting how their students will react to the ideas and exercises they are given to work with. Strategists and warriors use it for predicting how their opponents will respond to the perceived possibilities of a given time. The sword master Yagyū wrote on this subject in these terms:

> Removing afflictions is for the purpose of perceiving intentions. If afflictions are not removed, you will be distracted by them and fail to see. Fail to see and you've lost.
>
> "Afflictions" are illnesses of mind, meaning that the mind is dwelling on one point or another. The mind should be made not to dwell anywhere for so long as it takes to strike a blow. This is abandoning the mind without abandoning it.
>
> Seeing with the heart and mind is fundamental. It is only when you see from the heart and mind that your eyes catch on. So seeing with the eyes comes after seeing with the heart and mind. Seeing with the eyes, after that you should see with the body, hands, and feet.
>
> Affliction, or sickness, means to think obsessively about something. It is also sick to think obsessively about using the art of war. It is sick to think obsessively of showing what you have learned. It is sick to think only of attacking, and it is sick to think only of waiting. It is also sick to think obsessively about getting rid of sickness. When the mind dwells on anything exclusively, that is called sickness.
>
> Since all of these sicknesses are in the mind, the thing is to remove sickness and tune the mind.

Again, in his book of family traditions here Yagyū echoes the teaching of Zen master Takuan, who used Buddhist iconography to drive his point home. Citing the image of the Monarch of Immovable Light, traditionally portrayed as a warrior defending the Buddhist teaching, Takuan explains the meaning of the imperturbable Zen mind in action. He also uses the image of the Thousand-Handed Seeress, a personification of compassion whose "thousand hands" represent practical skills employed in the service of humanity and in liberating people from bondage to illusion. Takuan interprets this symbol in terms of the flexibility and versatility of the individual with an unfettered mind. In a letter to the swordsman Yagyū, the Zen master shows how these familiar icons illustrate practical exercises and attitudes applicable to the warrior's way:

> The Buddhist image of the Monarch of Immovable Light represents the state where one's unified mind does not move, which means not changing or upsetting oneself. Not changing or upsetting yourself means not dwelling on anything.
>
> Seeing things at a glance and not fixing the mind on them is called being unmoving. The reason for this is that when your mind lingers on things, various analytic thoughts take place in your heart, moving in various ways within your mind. When that stops, even if the lingering mind moves, you are nevertheless unmoved.
>
> For example, suppose ten people strike at you in succession. Parrying the first blow, if you do not let your mind linger on the impression, but take on one after another, leaving each behind as you go along, you will not be at loss to deal with all ten opponents. Although your mind works ten times with ten adversaries, if you don't let your mind linger on anyone, taking them on in turn, you won't be at a loss in action.
>
> Then again, if your mind lingers in front of one adversary, you might parry that one person's blow, but when the second opponent strikes you will fumble.
>
> There is another Buddhist image called the Thousand-Handed Seeress. If her mind stayed on one hand holding one particular tool, the other nine hundred and nintey-nine hands wouldn't work. It is because she doesn't keep her mind on one point that all of her hands are useful.
>
> Why would the Seeress have a thousand hands on just one body? This is a representation to show people that even if you have a thousand hands they are all useful once immovable wisdom is opened.
>
> If you gaze at a single leaf on a single tree, you do not see the other leaves. If you face the tree with no intention and don't fix your eyes on a single leaf, then you see all the many leaves. If your mind is preoccupied with one leaf, you don't see the others; if you don't set your attention on one, you see hundreds and

thousands of leaves. Someone who has understood this is actually the Seeress of a Thousand Hands and a Thousand Eyes.

A famous story illustrating this in practice is told of another Zen master of the late seventeenth century, popularly known as Shōjū Rōjin, the Old Man with Right Perception, an important yet little-known Zen master of premodern Japan.

According to his biographers, Shōjū Rōjin had been one of the bastard sons of a samurai family. As a youth at the age of thirteen he had become intensely introspective after an encounter with an old Zen monk. Several years later, he experienced what Zennists refer to as death and revitalization after an accident in which he temporarily lost consciousness. Subsequently he spent years looking for Buddhist teachers who could confirm his realization.

Eventually he met the Zen master Bunan and studied with him for eighteen years, until the master's death. Even with this experience, however, Shōjū Rōjin said that he did not achieve continuity in "right perception" until the age of fifty-five. Because of his emphasis on continuity of right perception, the clear seeing of a clear mind, the old man called his hermitage "The Hut of Right Perception" and was himself popularly known by the same name.

Very few professional Zennists ever found their way to the door of this old man, now one of the greatest masters in Japan, direct heir of an ancient lineage. Sometimes certain warriors, however, used to call on him for advice on clarification of mind. One day such a group was practicing Zen concentration by fencing in the master's view. When they paused, one of the warriors remarked to the Zen master, who was then a hermit, "As far as the principle is concerned, your understanding is superior to ours, but when it comes to actual fact, we are superior to you."

Seizing the opportunity to make a point, the old Zen master challenged the samurai swordsmen to hit him.

The warrior who had boasted of their skill handed the old man a wooden sword, but the Zen master refused, saying that as a Buddhist monk he would not handle any weapon, even an imitation. Instead, he said, he would use his fan, which had metal backings and could serve the purpose of defense. "Try to hit me," the old Zen man repeated, urging the samurai to strike.

The warriors could not refuse the challenge. Taking up their practice swords, they attacked the old man from every angle. Their wonderment grew and their stamina dwindled as they saw the old man give a virtuoso display of the special art of opposing a long sword with a dagger. Each and every blow the warriors struck was deftly parried by the Zen master's fan, which seemed to fly to the path of the swords like iron drawn to a magnet.

Finally exhausted, the warriors were forced to concede that the old man was fully able to turn his abstract knowledge into concrete action at will. One of them asked him how he did it. "Simple," the old Zen master replied; "when your objective perception is clear, you don't miss one out of ten thousand."

According to the understanding of the warrior Yagyū, there are two levels in the practice of removing sicknesses in the mind in order to attain the clarity that would enable one to act this accurately and effectively in the midst of events. In his book of family traditions, he describes the first level in these terms:

> The first level is where you get into thought yet have no thoughts, get into attachments yet have no attachments: this means that thinking of removing of sickness is thought. To think of getting rid of sicknesses in the mind is to get involved in thought.
>
> Sickness means obsessive thought. To think of getting rid of sickness is also thought. Therefore you use thought to get rid of thoughts. When you get rid of thoughts, that is called having no thoughts. This is why we speak of getting into thought having no thoughts.
>
> When you take thought to get rid of the sickness that remains in thought, after that the thought of removal and the thoughts to be removed all become nothing together. This is what is known as using a wedge to remove a wedge.
>
> When you can't get a wedge out, if you drive another one in so as to ease the tightness the first wedge comes out. Once the stuck wedge comes out, the wedge driven in afterwards no longer remains there.
>
> When sickness is gone, the thought of getting rid of sickness no longer remains, so this is called getting into thought to have no thought.
>
> To think of getting rid of sickness is to be attached to sickness, but if you use that attachment to get rid of sickness, the attachment won't remain; so this is called getting into attachment to have no attachment.

According to the classical Chinese Zen master Baizhang, as long as there is deliberate practice and realization in Zen, the teaching is still incomplete. It is only after having transcended the steps of practice and attainment that the complete teaching is realized. Wansong, a later Chinese master, summarized this in a proverb: "It is easy to advance with every step; it is hard to let go of each state of mind." Following the Zen teaching, the Japanese swordsman Yagyū defines the advanced level of his art in terms of spontaneity and natural freedom.

> In the advanced level, getting rid of sickness means having no thought whatsoever of getting rid of sickness. To think of riddance is itself sickness. To let sickness be while living in the midst of sickness is to be rid of sickness.
>
> Thinking of getting rid of sickness happens because sickness is still in the mind. Therefore sickness doesn't leave at all, and whatever you do and think is done with attachment, so there can be no higher value in it.
>
> Masters of the arts cannot be called adepts as long as they have not left behind attachment to their various skills.

The *Tao Te Ching,* a Taoist classic studied in Zen master Takuan's school, says that "the great adept seems as if inept." While this may outwardly resemble humility as ordinarily understood, in esoteric tradition it is at once a protective device and a means of keeping the mind clear of exaggerated self-importance, which is in Buddhist terms a "sickness" that screens consciousness from objective perception.

A common conception of the detachment of the Zen outlook is that it constitutes the goal of practice and is itself the liberation proposed by Buddhism. Classical masters openly deny this, teaching that detachment is properly speaking an avenue of extra perception and extra opportunity. Original Zen literature abounds with criticisms of practitioners who rest in detachment for their own comfort and do not employ it for constructive development.

In the work of the warrior Musashi, it becomes clear that the clarification of mind for which elementary Zen practice is designed becomes as it were a door to enhanced performance. In his *Book of Five Spheres,* Musashi stresses the importance of perceptive discernment not only in the warrior's way but in all walks of life, to gain an objective understanding of the mechanisms of timing and success.

There is rhythm in everything, but the rhythms of the art of war are especially difficult to master without practice. . . . There are also rhythms in the ups and downs of all careers. . . . Carefully distinguish the rhythm of rise and decline in all things. . . . In battle, the way to win is to know opponents' rhythms while using unexpected rhythms yourself, producing formless rhythms from the rhythms of wisdom.

The necessary practicality of the warrior's way tended to prevent followers of the martial arts from becoming mere Zen cultists, even if it did not stop similar involutionary trends from taking place within their own specialty. Musashi's obsession with martial arts seems to have been mainly responsible for the relative shallowness of his Zen realization; or it may be the other way about, based on something in Musashi's early personality development.

Musashi did nevertheless attempt to establish a theoretical and practical basis for rounding out the personality of the warrior, in a manner characteristic of the later Neo-Confucian schools under the influence of Zen Buddhism. This effort can be seen in his own cultural pursuits, and above all in the introduction to his own famous treatise on strategy and the martial arts, where he outlines a general program for the overall mental development of the individual warrior.

1. Think of what is right and true.
2. Put the science into practice.
3. Become acquainted with the arts.
4. Become acquainted with the crafts.
5. Understand the negative and positive qualities in everything.
6. Learn to see everything accurately.
7. Become aware of what is not obvious.
8. Be careful even in small matters.
9. Don't do anything useless.

THE WAY OF THE ZEN WARRIOR

Throughout the strife-torn Middle Ages of feudal Japan, people in all walks of life were experimenting with Zen learning to master the essence of their own way. Some of the Zen masters were themselves warriors; others were intellectuals, farmers, artisans, merchants, physicians, soothsayers, vagrants, and outcastes. Some might be all of these things in the course of a lifetime.

When the prolonged Warring States era ended around the year 1600, a movement began to recollect and systematize the scattered arts and sciences of that turbulent yet strangely brilliant era. Modern knowledge of the traditional arts and sciences, including Zen and the way of the warrior, is largely based on elaborations of those reconstructed and systematized versions of ancient knowledge.

Yagyū Munenori and Miyamoto Musashi were extraordinary warriors who lived through a historical watershed in Japanese civilization. In their works they employed an ancient core of educational techniques and learning methods to play their part in the adaptation of the culture to a new historical climate. The peculiarity of their particular role as warriors was that war no longer existed for them, for all that were left were administrative and police functions.

Under those conditions, the need for danger to use the warrior's way as a means of self-perfection could easily become a menace to society. For warriors like Musashi, this need became an obsession with dueling itself, which eventually seemed to prevent him from fully realizing Zen. It is not easy to tell whether in the end Musashi himself knew whether he had studied Zen to master the art of war, or whether he had studied the art of war to master Zen. They say that he died of an ulcer, aggravated beyond measure by years of fanatic austerities.

This solitary struggle was undoubtedly a major factor in the formation of Musashi's thought and writing on warriorhood, with its particular attention to strategic detail and methodical approach. His injunctions on learning typify this characteristic, simple yet inclusive, summarizing both Buddhist and Confucian principles of learning in

a manner that is easy to remember and that, like the classics themselves, yields more with time and reflection.

One reason for Musashi's interest in basic education was, as he
himself wrote, that "particularly in this science one can fall into
perversions through even a little bit of misperception of the way, or
confusion about the way." Yagyū also considered learning important
but at the same time stressed two points: that its function within the
total design of the way is preparatory; and that it is to be distinguished
from mere intellectualism.

> Learning is the gate, not the house. When you see the gate,
> don't think it is the house. You have to go through the gate to
> get to the house, which is behind it.
>
> Since learning is a gate, when you read books don't think this
> is the Way. This misconception has made many people remain
> ignorant of the Way no matter how much they study and how
> many words they know.

This is characteristic of the Zen attitude toward learning, which is
judged by function and utility, not by appearance. The original
Buddhist teaching applies this to all kinds of learning, both conventional and sacred. One of the main thrusts of Zen teaching is to
dethrone intellectual knowledge from its status as a personal appurtenance. According to *The Flower Ornament Scripture*, one of the
all-time favorite texts of Zen teachers, "Like someone counting others'
treasures without half a coin of his own: so is the one who is learned
but does not apply the teaching. Like someone on a corner saying all
kinds of fine things, but with no real virtue inside: so are those who
do not practice."

Eventually this outlook was carried over into other schools of
thought, which tended to become more universal and more pragmatic
under the influence of Zen, which had originally developed in China
out of a distillation of the essences of all the Buddhist teachings. This
naturally included the "outside" teachings belonging to host cultures
as they were absorbed and employed by Buddhists in their missionary
activity. This is illustrated by the Japanese Zen master Takuan, who
identifies several schools of learning in terms of a common underlying
aim rather than distinguishing them in terms of external cultural
differences. This aim, in turn, he identifies with the essence of Zen.

> Although Shintō, poetics, and Confucianism are various in their
> ways, all of them speak of the clarification of the universal mind.

It is to be expected that there are people in this world who don't know the mind. Those who do understand it are rarely seen. And even if someone does clearly know, it is still hard to put into practice. Even if you can talk about the universal mind, that doesn't mean you understand mind.

Even though Buddhism and Confucianism both talk about mind, the mind without the personal conduct implied is something that is not clearly known—if you do not practice the teaching, you do not really know it. As long as people don't seriously investigate the origin of mind and come to realize it, they do not understand; it is not clear to them.

It is important to realize here that the schools of Shintō, poetics, and Confucianism to which Zen master Takuan refers as having a common theme are not their original forms, but are special developments that took place under the impact of Zen. Takuan is therefore not referring not simply to his own subjective appreciation of these various ways, but also to historical facts in the history of their development.

Confucianism had already been assimilated to Zen in China five hundred years earlier, while certain types of Shintō and Japanese poetics (which were already closely related disciplines from their very origin) were strongly influenced by Zen Buddhism in medieval Japan. During the seventeenth century, in the time of Takuan, Yagyū, and Musashi, it was customary for Zen masters to speak as if Buddhism, Confucianism, and Shintō were basically identical in spirit.

In both theory and practice there are, of course, many counter-examples to this generalization, but the Zen swordsman Yagyū pursued the unitarian theme even further than his teacher Takuan had in their correspondence. In defining adepthood, Yagyū found the ultimate unity to be in the combination of essence and totality, and in this he follows the root teaching of *The Flower Ornament Scripture* rather than a sectarian Zen line such as would be formulated in the following century. Because this is not an undefined or undifferentiated unity, while on the one hand Yagyū regarded the boundaries between fields of thought and action as real only in appearance and not in essence, on the other hand he acknowledged general distinctions of universality versus hyperspecialization or sectarianism, and genuineness versus imitation. In his book on family tradition he wrote:

Those who master one skill or one art are called expert in their particular ways, but that is not to be called complete adepthood.

There is also imitation Zen. A lot of people say similar things that are not really the right path. So people who are supposedly Zennists are not all the same.

There are people who preach that mind is empty, but people who realize this clearly are rare.

The emptiness of mind is not visible to the eye, but do not think that it is nothing: once this mind-emptiness moves it does all kinds of things. The action of the hands and feet, however varied and skilled, all are accomplished from the movement of this emptiness, this mind.

It is hard to really understand this mind by reading books or listening to talks. People who have written and spoken about it since olden times have just written and spoken in standard terms; rare are they who have attained the way mind-to-mind.

The mood of total detachment means to detach from all sorts of afflictions at once. Afflictions are afflictions of mind. This means that you make all the various afflictions in your mind into one, and lightheartedly detach from the whole bunch.

Generally speaking, affliction means fixation of the mind. In Buddhism this is called attachment, and it is considered extremely undesirable. If the mind sticks to one place and dwells on it, you fail to see what there is to see and unexpectedly lose.

The challenge for the student of Zen and Zen arts, therefore, was to distinguish the levels of practitioners: there were the complete adepts, who were masters of both Zen and art; the experts, who knew enough Zen to master an art, or who knew one art to the threshold of Zen; the dilettantes, who tried to imitate the externals of the experts for their own amusement; and the charlatans, who imitated experts for their own profit. Generally speaking, they could be distinguished by the specific spheres or fixations of attention governing their lives, but only if people trying to assess them had no personal prejudices of their own. For this reason the Zen interest in objective knowledge was reflected in a Zen interest in the educational process itself.

Suzuki Shōsan, a contemporary warrior turned Zennist who went even further than Musashi and Yagyū in educational work, was not just an individual dueling artist like those two warriors, but earlier in life had actually fought in war. Like many victorious warriors, Shōsan had given up arms when peacetime came, and even in his most chilling

Zen writings does not display the murderous fanaticism or give off the scent of blood that marks the work of Musashi, the perpetual competitor.

Shōsan's work is still no less cutting than Musashi's, even on the level of mundane realities; and the ex-commander Shōsan also demonstrates a purer and more articulate understanding of Zen and the other spiritual ways than does the idiosyncratic dueler Musashi. Like many other disarmed warriors, Shōsan also later worked as a healer, even successfully reviving an ancient method of spiritual curing. In spite of its lofty idealism, his approach to education is therefore extremely perceptive and sympathetic to the particular needs of the individual as well as to the needs engendered by the general currents of behaviors and events.

Shōsan deflated the sort of thinking that conceived of Zen awakening as a magical cure-all, and that thought of Zen practice as a sort of training applied *to* the person. In this he followed classical Zen teaching, which maintained that the evolutionary transformation of the individual had to come from within to permeate the whole mind and behavior. Unless inner change is effective, according to ancient teachers, external disciplines can have a reverse influence on the self and promote such dangerous qualities as arrogance and insensitivity.

One of the first Zen principles of learning is summed up in the proverb, "Gazing at the moon in the sky, you lose the pearl in your hands." A Chinese proverb also says, "Hurry, and you won't arrive." The early Japanese Zen master Dōgen, a long-neglected pioneer of native Zen literature in Japan and one of Suzuki Shōsan's major inspirations, expressed this in a poem:

> Dig the pond
> Without waiting for the moon.
> When the pond is finished,
> the moon will come by itself.

Shōsan followed many of Dōgen's teachings, and also spoke of Buddhism as something that could be practiced at any given moment without being inhibited by remote aspirations.

> People today think that Buddhism is useless if you don't become enlightened. This is not right. Buddhism means using your present mind well, so it is of immediate usefulness. Buddhist practice is using your mind as strongly as possible. As your mind becomes stronger, it gradually becomes more useful.

Shōsan further stressed the negative effects of exaggeration and impatience in both ordinary and spiritual pursuits; he observed, "Those who have gone to hell because of the world can be saved by Buddhism, but what can save those who have gone to hell because of Buddhism?" Therefore he emphasized the importance of right orientation in the practice of a discipline.

> Beginners undertaking a discipline should see to it that they themselves are genuinely sincere. People should not force themselves to do any discipline without being really genuine. If you exert yourself unreasonably or undergo austerities, you will exhaust yourself and diminish your potential, all to no avail.
>
> When your psychological state is bad, disciplines will just make it worse. Discipline is a matter of fortifying potential, so it is imperative to avoid depletion.
>
> Nowadays countless people have depleted their potential and become ill or insane by practicing discipline wrongly or doing imitation Zen meditation. One should just develop one's will and become truly genuine.

These warnings strike a note different from that of popularizers who portray meditation as something that is good for everyone, at any time. There is no lack of contemporary examples of psychological and physical ailments such as those Shōsan mentions occurring in practitioners of meditation, fostered or exacerbated by the grafting of "spiritual" techniques onto an unsuitable basis.

In the West this has often been attributed to cultural differences, but the same problem exists in the East, as Shōsan's own remarks bear witness, and madness also occurs in native Japanese Zen schools, particularly those in which certain practices are routinely performed under intensive pressure without regard to traditional caveats such as those mentioned here by Suzuki Shōsan. Mental disturbance of some kind seems to be particularly common in stories of Japanese Zen monks of the last hundred years, an especially trying time for traditionalized Zen as a whole. This was also exacerbated by the fragmentation of Buddhist sects, which preserved fixed forms of practice in isolation from the total context of Buddhism.

In a typically Buddhist fashion, Suzuki Shōsan's teachings were cast in different styles to address the specific problems and mentalities of the various stations of life in his society. Although increasing numbers of children from among the farmers, artisans, and merchants were soon to learn reading and writing through the work of local Buddhist grammar schools, in Shōsan's time and for centuries thereafter the warriors were the most educated class in Japan. Therefore those of his talks and writings directed specifically to warriors contain the most advice on the subject of education and character development. Again characteristically Buddhist in this sense, these works of Zen master Suzuki Shōsan are a mine of quotations that are useful even in their most obvious meanings, and yield more as experience and understanding deepen:

> Stand up and be responsible for yourself. Even people who are prudent in everything will hide their secret faults when they are only concerned about public opinion and outward appearances. So even very conventional and conservative people will have faults in their inner minds. Beware of your mind, and take responsibility for yourself.

This contrasts sharply with the image of Japanese morality as fundamentally other-directed. Ordinarily shame is considered the operative element in ruling Japanese social behaviors; but here Shōsan illustrates the shortcomings of shame in comparison with conscience, with which it was originally linked in Buddhist psychotherapeutics. Western Christian moral feeling and Japanese moral feeling are commonly compared in terms of a distinction between guilt and shame. By pairing shame and conscience, in contrast, traditional Buddhist psychology includes both social and personal moral feelings in a continuum of consciousness. Shōsan also shows how the inward personal experience of being directly affects the outward interpersonal experience. The kind of Zen introspection and self-knowledge Shōsan teaches is therefore not a form of self-involvement to distract one from external realities, but is in evident fact a way to survey the foundation of ordinary social psychology and the roots of social behavior.

> Be aware of yourself and know yourself. No matter how much you have learned and how much you know, if you don't know yourself you don't know anything. Indeed, if you don't know yourself you cannot know anything else.
>
> People who don't know themselves criticize others from the point of view of their own ignorant selves. They consider what-

ever agrees with them to be good, and hate whatever doesn't go their way. They become irritated about everything, causing themselves to suffer by themselves, bothering themselves solely because of their own prejudices.

If you know that not everyone will be agreeable to you, know that you won't be agreeable to everyone either. Those who have no prejudices in themselves do not reject people, and therefore people do not reject them.

Buddhist philosophy and psychology are based on logical and experiential relativity of subject and object. Therefore objectivity is approached through analytic criticism combined with inner exercises to minimize the influence of subjectivity, in order to develop the ability to outmaneuver self-deceptive biases. According to Zen master Dōgen, "Studying Buddhism is studying self. To study the self is to forget self. To forget self is to be enlightened by all things."

In this Zen context, self-study not only means investigation into the real self, it also means learning about the subjective biases of false selves. Forgetting self means penetrating the barrier of self-deception by a false self. Being enlightened by all things is direct learning through the experiences of life as it is, without the mythology of false selves imposing their judgments and preconceptions on what it means to be.

Shōsan goes on to describe the attitude of detached yet intentional self-monitoring. This is used in Buddhist practice to overcome unnecessary limitations imposed on the capacity and function of mind by unchecked wandering:

> Developmental exercise is a matter of being as strongminded as possible. Our conditioned senses and ideas are like bandits that can steal our original mind. These bandits arise from weakness in our minds. Therefore you should use your energy strongly to watch intently over your own mind. People misunderstand the Zen term "no thought" and use it to become absentminded dolts. This is a big mistake. You should keep a strong mind.

The misunderstanding of "no thought" to which Shōsan refers would appear to have plagued Zen movements over the centuries, from earliest times to the present day. Sometimes there is no one like Shōsan around to point out that this is not Zen, and the aberration has been mistaken for the real thing. This polarizes the uninformed public exposed to such a movement, in a manner that is not entirely useful either to those who accept Zen or those who reject Zen on this basis.

Misunderstanding has at times reached the point where irrationality has come to be considered the measure of Zen, not only by opponents but even by proponents. Many of the incoherent utterances of modern popularizers such as D. T. Suzuki and C. G. Jung testify to the existence of this phenomenon in the present day.

Somewhat less flamboyant than the irrationalists are the quietists, who also have appeared from time to time and who have earned for Zen a reputation of social irrelevance at best and parasitism at worst. Shōsan was among the foremost of those to counter these negative images with the assertion and demonstration that Zen mind is not blank, otherworldly, or irrational, but in fact eminently practical in ordinary life.

> Buddhist practice means eliminating obstacles caused by historical events, thus getting rid of all misery. This mind is a treasure that brings physical and mental peace and happiness to all classes and occupations when used in their lives.
>
> Buddhist practice is eliminating foul, polluted attitudes, becoming pure and unblocked in mind, turning misery to happiness, turning evil to good. This mind is a treasure useful in all undertakings and all good works.
>
> Buddhist practice is eliminating confused and ignorant attitudes, so as to be beyond greed, hatred, and delusion. This mind is a treasure of mental health that ends psychological afflictions.

Far from being irrational, Zen teaching points out the irrationality of a life dominated by instincts and emotions. One of the first steps of Buddhist practice is to take stock of the effect that compulsions have on the individual, and how this makes one internally and externally vulnerable to control by unmanageable forces.

> Fools disregard their lives for the sake of desires. Even though they trouble themselves mentally and physically by their cravings, they are never satisfied; and yet they never give up.

Buddhism teaches ways of transcending compulsion and attaining freedom through "forgetting the self," in Zen master Dōgen's words. This does not mean that there is no awareness of self, only that awareness is not enclosed in any self. The enlightenment attributed to buddhas includes awareness of all selves, including actual and possible selves as well as the "self of selves." This naturally includes what are ordinarily thought of as the selves of others, which means that the individual aware of the selves of others is also aware of the selves of self. Shōsan therefore distinguishes among practical qualities and scales of remembrance and forgetfulness of self.

Shōsan makes it clear that to forget the self does not mean to act impulsively or irrationally, or to live with heedless abandon. In the same way that he warns people against exaggerated misunderstanding of the technique of "no thought," Shōsan is careful to balance a reasonable practice of self-forgetting with a conscientious practice of self-awareness. In this way the individual is centered between extremes, neither too involved with self nor too careless of self.

> Forget yourself, yet don't forget yourself. When people are ambitious and greedy, they are concerned exclusively with themselves, forgetting even their own relatives. On the other hand, when in pursuit of what they like they forget themselves and lose their conscience, so they do not understand the implications of what they do and are unconcerned about even the direst of consequences. Much unworthy behavior derives from this, so don't forget yourself.

Following traditional Zen Buddhist teaching, Shōsan explains further that self-indulgence is not confined to what is ordinarily thought of as selfish or immoral behavior, but also infects activity that is conventionally considered good or virtuous.

> There is contaminated goodness, and there is uncontaminated goodness. What is done without self-consciousness is called uncontaminated goodness. What is done for your own sake, in hopes of reward, is called contaminated goodness.

Ancient Zen masters have in fact said that self-centered virtue can be even worse than self-centered vice. Piety does not call down on itself the opprobrium of conventional society, because it is clothed in acceptable appearances; therefore the unreflective individual is not put under any pressure to reexamine personal behavior and its subjective interpretations. Under these conditions it is much easier to become set in one's ways, fortified by a self-perpetuating circle of rationalizations and justifications.

For these reasons, fluidity and nonattachment are considered essential prerequisites for attainment of a perspective comprehensive enough to assess the purpose and effect of behaviors, whether secular or sacred, in the objective light of its total context. The martial artists preach detachment for the purpose of mastering their special skills, and in a sense the warrior who has suffered a mortal defeat in battle may have nothing else but detachment as an ultimate resort, a final personal victory. As a Buddhist wayfarer, Shōsan also faces the reality of death, but he extends the principle of fluidity to an art of progressive living.

> There is virtue in not stagnating. People get fixated at one point or another, with the result that they are unaware of what went before or what comes after. Thus they lack virtue. In their livelihood as well as in their perceptions of others, they often lose much for a little gain. They are, however, unaware of this in themselves. So if you want to leave the small for the great, notice your fixations and detach from them.

Even apart from the awareness of death obligatory for professional warriors, remembrance of impermanence and the inevitability of personal death has been used by Buddhists in all walks of life as one of the most accessible and efficient methods of freeing the mind from compulsive attachment to things. This is one of the basic exercises of elementary Buddhist practice, found throughout the broad spectrum of Buddhist schools and scriptures.

Early Western investigators who became fixated on this particular type of practice and treated it in isolation from the greater tradition of unitarian Buddhism were naturally horrified by this consciousness of death and consequently portrayed Buddhism as a pessimistic religion. Far from being morbid, as emotional Western critics have claimed, this aspect of Buddhism actually enables practitioners to appreciate life more fully, to be freer and more efficient in whatever they do. It also teaches them to meet sickness and death serene and unafraid.

This is in any case just one part of a much larger teaching, and the emphasis given to death by professional soldiers over centuries of warfare in medieval Japan should not be considered the measure of Buddhist consciousness. There is something very positive in the immediate awareness of evanescence, something that is neither in the grim stoicism of the warrior in the field nor in the wistful pining of the poet in a garden. Shōsan explains how the tendency to forget or ignore transitoriness affects the whole mood and conduct of life.

> When people forget that they are going to die, and act as if they think they are going to live forever, they do not fully appreciate and utilize the passing months and years. As long as they are like this, they only act on greed, anger, and falsehood, turning away from social and family duties, not understanding human kindness and obligation, employing flattery and cajolery, neglecting home and work for useless hobbies and amusements.

Shōsan's Zen is rooted in the practicalities of earthly life. He had no time for airy-fairy "spirituality" divorced from the needs of everyday existence. Even the extraordinary phenomena of enhanced intellect and psychic powers were made by Shōsan to serve common needs such as education and healing. His intellectual and practical amalgamation of social and Buddhist teachings is summarized in an essay "On the Daily Life of Warriors," which is not meant for professional samurai alone, but is intended as a model for responsible people in all walks of life.

> A samurai asked, "They say Buddhist principles and social principles are like the two wheels of a chariot. But even if there is no Buddhism, that does not imply any lack in the world. Why are the two sets of principles likened to the twin wheels of a chariot?"
>
> Shōsan answered, "Buddhist principles and social principles are not two separate things. According to a Buddhist saying, 'If you can enter the world successfully, you are totally beyond the world.'"

To say that ability to enter the world successfully means ability to transcend the world means that efficiency reduces confusion, thus freeing mental energy from preoccupation with matters pending. In contrast to this, premature attempts to get "beyond the world" solely by supposedly "spiritual" exercises can result in slovenly management of daily and long-term affairs, which then increases ordinary anxieties. This in turn has the effect of hindering freedom of mind, closing the open end of life and thus adding spiritual anxiety to preexisting worries about things of the world. The result of this is that neither side of human life, the mundane or the spiritual, receives its due attention, as that due to the one is given to the other and vice versa.

Part of the problem connected with images of irrationality in Zen comes from the definition of rationality with which the interpreter starts. If the modern alliance of warfare and science is considered rational, or the product of rational thinking, it would not be any wonder that someone from modern Japan like D. T. Suzuki would want to throw a monkey-wrench into that machine and at least try to slow it down by touting irrationality to its intellectuals, writing extensively on Zen stories hand-picked for their apparently puzzling character.

Even a scholar and psychologist of the status of C. G. Jung admits to an inability to discern the symbolic meanings of the Zen stories related by D. T. Suzuki in a book to which Jung himself wrote an introduction in 1939. This image of inscrutability was to become one of the hallmarks of the popular Western image of Zen. It was hardly suspected that this might not be an altogether veridical image. Even less considered was the possibility that this mysteriousness was of a strategic rather than essential nature.

Now that these dimensions of behavior have become of concern in the arenas of commercial and political activities, and because Zen has also become commercialized and politicized, there has developed more academic interest in corresponding aspects of Zen. Although there are many outlines and discussions, however, nothing really like a comprehensive study of the subject is yet available.

What the ordinary person in search of information may be most likely to find are books representing particular teachings, sects, or schools; books on the personal experiences of individuals practicing some kind of Zen exercise; or academic tomes on some relic of the past. Many treatments of Zen do in fact contain irrational elements, largely based on personal attachments to what Zen Buddhists themselves call the "traces."

In contrast to irrational or superficial Zennists envisioned through commercialized or propagandistic versions of the teaching, who in view of their mention in Zen literature obviously are not unique anywhere and must exist in all times and places side by side with truth, Shōsan teaches Buddhism in a way that clearly shows its foundation of reason, starting from the premise that "both Buddhist and social principles are nothing but the application of genuine honesty, making reasoning accurate and action just."

This formulation is a typical example of a concrete reflection of the "nonduality" principle as it is understood in Buddhist philosophy. Shōsan can sincerely say that social virtues and Buddhist virtues are one, yet can still distinguish differences in how the same virtues are understood and practiced on different levels of consciousness.

> There are different levels of depth in honesty. Honesty in the social context means not twisting reason, being dutiful and just, giving all social relations their proper attention, harmonizing with others, and being unselfish and fair. This is a way to enter from a relatively shallow dimension into a deeper dimension.

It is a commonplace of Buddhism that social ethics serve as a preparation for the higher psychological development fostered by spiritual practices. This does not diminish the dignity or importance of social ethics, but places them in a broader context than religious dogmatics. One of the great advantages of the wider view of Buddhism is that it reduces the human tendency to stagnate morally through self-righteousness or cynicism. Shōsan exemplifies this as he describes the deeper meaning of honesty in typical Buddhist metaphysical terms.

> Honesty in the context of Buddhism is to realize that all fabricated things are ultimately unreal deceptions, and thus to use the original spiritual body in oneself in its natural spontaneous state.

Here the difficulty of Zen for the pedestrian mind becomes evident. The prospect of being able to utilize a "spiritual body in oneself" may appeal to the ordinary interest in advantage of any kind; but there is still a socially ingrained resistance to the idea that conventionally structured experiences and institutions are ultimately unreal. To ordinary conception, this notion would seem destructive, but Shōsan illustrates how it works in the total context of Buddhism, as a doorway to liberation of creative potential.

In Buddhist terms, the ultimate unreality of mundane things does not mean that they are insignificant or negligible, but rather that they are malleable, which means that they are workable. Realization of emptiness therefore does not mean withdrawal from the world, but rather the capacity for change, the potential for progress. Shōsan goes on to describe the kind of change and progress for which Zen Buddhism aims as it heals the "mental illnesses" that keep humans immersed in animalistic behaviors. Here the intimate connection between individual liberation and collective liberation is made obvious.

Ordinary people are mortally ill; buddhas are master physicians. Ordinary people should first of all get rid of their illnesses. In the fluctuating and unenlightened mind, there are the illnesses of delusion and confusion; there are the illnesses of greed and misperception; there are the illnesses of cowardice and injustice. Based on the mind full of the poisons of greed, hatred, and delusion, these poisons produce eighty-four thousand mental illnesses. Getting rid of this mind is called Buddhism. Is this any different from the principle of society?

The Buddhist teaching on the objective unreality or emptiness of conditioned phenomena was typically made a prime target of anti-Buddhist invective both East and West, by those who misconstrued the doctrine as a form of nihilism or quietism. While it is true that some neurotic Zennists with escapist tendencies were greatly attracted to a nihilistic view of emptiness, orthodox Buddhist tradition has always repudiated such exaggerations as perversions. According to Nāgārjuna, a spiritual ancestor of Zen in India and one of the greatest writers on the metaphysics of emptiness, "The enlightened have said that emptiness is departure from all views, but they have also said that those who make emptiness a view cannot be saved."

Shōsan makes it clear that realization of emptiness is not the goal of Zen, but the means by which to eliminate biased views and undesirable psychological complexes rooted in deceptions about the nature of reality. He contrasts the freedom gained through practical use of emptiness with the bondage resulting from fixation on appearances.

> Knowing the principle of original emptiness, those who have mastered the Way use reason and justice as a forge to temper the mind daily, getting rid of impurities to turn it into a pure, clear, unopposed mind-sword, which cuts through the thought-root of selfish greed and conquers all thoughts, so that the Way-farers ride on top of everything, untroubled by anything, beginningless and endless.

> But ordinary people take deceptions for realities, creating attitudes biased by fixation on appearances, thus starting up thoughts of craving, anger, and misunderstanding. Having produced all sorts of psychological afflictions and lost the original mind, they find that their minds are distracted and unfocused, giving in to whatever thoughts arise. As a result of this, they

suffer from handicapped mentalities that make them hurt. They have no psychological buoyancy; they are gloomy and depressed, living aimlessly and without self-understanding, fixating their attention on things. This is called the mentality of the common man.

The distinction made in Zen between ordinary people and enlightened people is not based on formal accomplishments but on the level of mind in which their everyday lives are grounded. Shōsan describes the mentality of the common man as chronically superficial, fixated on appearances and attached to things. This is thought of as a loss, or alienation from the autonomy of the "original mind," which Zen teaching identifies with "buddha nature."

The primary desideratum of Zen is to recover the experience of original mind through itself. From this standpoint it is possible to see through the deception of attachment to superficialities. Shōsan explains the practical qualities of original mind as experienced in Zen, with emphasis on the psychological freedom and security attained through its penetrating insight and autonomy.

We should know different names for the original mind. It is called the indestructible true substance, or the stable spiritual body. This mind is not caught up in things, is not fearful or alarmed, does not worry or withdraw. Imperturbable and unchanging, it becomes the master of everything. Those who have penetrated this and can actually use it are called great sturdy folk, people with hearts and guts of steel, or people who have attained the Way. People like this, unimpeded by all thoughts, can freely employ all things, events, and situations.

Because of the persistent tendency of the superficial mentality to cling to externals, the discipline needed to free the energy of mind from entanglements cannot really be imposed on the individual from without, but must come from within. In the absence of corresponding inner strength, outward discipline itself becomes an attachment, an appurtenance of the ego, leading to the kind of cultism and sentimental religiosity so often encountered in self-proclaimed spiritual coteries. Shōsan's own background made no allowance for make-believe discipline; he was therefore adamant in his insistence on the necessity of inner strength and independent will power.

So people who practice the way of buddhas first need to have courage and intensity of purpose; otherwise it is hard to succeed.

It is impossible to enter the way of buddhas with a timid heart. If you do not protect yourself surely and cultivate yourself strongly, you will suffer from whatever mental afflictions occur.

Those who use a firm heart and a stable mind to overcome all things are called people of the Way. Those whose thoughts stick to appearances and who thus suffer miserably, at the mercy of events, are called ordinary people.

Shōsan's attitude would seem to be characteristic of a warrior, and he did bring his experience in military training and combat to bear on the issues of Zen psychology in dealing with the general problems of life and death. Yet he was careful to distinguish the "courage" required of the independent Zen mind from the "courage" of warriors associated with force and violence.

So people who stir up the courage of bloodlust with afflicted minds may at some point have the force to break through iron walls, but there is inevitably a time when bloodlust is exhausted and moods change. A sturdy heart, in contrast, is immovable and does not change. If warriors cultivate it, why wouldn't they develop such a sturdy heart?

If they have afflicted minds, even people of tremendous martial valor will find that when they face the end of their lives and the killer ghost of impermanence comes after them, their usual forcefulness will run out, their courageous ferocity will be gone, and they will be unable to muster any strength.

The distinction between the animal ferocity of the armed warrior killing opponents and the spiritual ferocity of the Zen warrior cutting through illusions was not always remembered and observed by Zennists following the practices of schools influenced by or oriented toward the life of the Japanese samurai. Even today one can hear and read seemingly endless tales of physical and mental violence in certain Rinzai Zen monasteries, as if this sort of fierceness were a measure of the quality of their discipline.

All too often this brand of samurai machismo is tied to the same superficial mechanism of self-importance that deludes the ordinary mentality. As a result of this the ego is not transcended but aggrandized and hardened by the discipline to which it is trained. Shōsan therefore made it clear that the cultivation of moral fiber in the Buddhist sense centers on dispelling the illusions created by self-importance.

The root source of misery is the thought, "Me, me." To know this is so is reason. Acting on knowledge of this reason with a mind of true courage, only justice can extirpate that thought.

People without reason do not understand the source of misery and happiness; people without justice cannot cut the halter of life and death. This calls for close attention.

As in his interpretation of "honesty," here again Shōsan uses Buddhistic understanding of "reason" and "justice" that penetrate more deeply than the commonplace Confucian definitions of these terms. In Shōsan's time, an academic form of Neo-Confucianism was officially adopted as state orthodoxy, but this doctrine typically suffered from a tendency to lapse into sterile intellectualism without practical means of empowering its principles. Therefore most Confucian scholars without political ambitions were more inclined toward the unorthodox versions of Neo-Confucianism that contained more of the pragmatic elements of Buddhism.

Drawing on both Zen and Neo-Confucian teachings, Shōsan concludes his essay on the daily life of warriors with a discussion on ways of developing the strength of character he deemed so important for both social and spiritual life. He contrasts attitudes or moods of what he calls a buoyant mind that rises above mundane conditions with depressive states of mind that are overcome by mundane conditions.

In the mind of the ordinary person there are buoyant moods when they overcome things, and there are depressed moods when they are overcome by things. Use of buoyant moods is a way into the world of enlightenment; use of depressed moods is a way into prison. Concentrating the power of aspiration for liberation, one should keep a buoyant mood day and night.

Here are buoyant moods that overcome things by means of a courageous mind: mindfulness of life and death; gratitude for blessings; indomitability in making progress; awareness of causality; insight into unreality and impermanence; respect for the value of time; watchfulness over oneself; self-abandon; self-criticism; respectfulness; humanitarian justice; attention to the sayings of the enlightened; kindness, compassion, uprightness, and honesty; reflection on what is most important.

Such states of mind come from a courageous and firm mind, so they leave off all sorts of attachments and rise above things.

Therefore when you maintain a buoyant state of mind you will suffer but little even if you suddenly go to your death.

When this courageous attitude is continuous, the citadel of the heart is secure, with virtuous power that is unhindered and independent. Even if all sorts of bewilderments should arise, they cannot face up to this firm heart; they will lose their force and disappear when their energy is gone. Should warriors not have such a firm heart?

If you are weakminded and your thoughts are fixed on appearances, bewilderments get power over you with increasing force, invading your nature, confusing your mind, and making you lose control of yourself.

There are also depressive moods that are overcome by things: negligence; tourism, incivility; indifference to consequences; disregard for the facts of impermanence and unreality; desire for fame and fortune; luxury; doubt and distrust; stickiness; timidity; merciless stinginess and greed; jealousy and envy; ingratitude; obsequiousness; heedlessness of life and death.

In contrast to Suzuki Shōsan's detailed explanation of Zen in the warrior's way, Zen master Takuan's instructions to the martial artist Yagyū Munenori all hinge upon the central principle of fluidity. It is also possible to interpret many of Suzuki's sayings as elaborations of this principle in practice, and even Takuan's tightly centered writings draw a great deal of practical wisdom from this simple premise. The characteristic beauty of Takuan's writings is their insistent return to fundamentals, one of the hallmarks of Zen.

The first of Takuan's letters to Yagyū recorded in the collection entitled *Writings on the Wonders of Immovable Knowledge* is entitled "The Affliction of Unaware Fixation." Here he introduces the topic of Zen perception in the context of dueling, symbolic of human confrontation, contention, and conflict.

In terms of the art of war, when you see an opponent's sword slashing at you, if you think to parry it then and there, your mind fixes on the sword. Then your action falters and you get cut by your adversary. This is called fixation, or lingering.

If you don't set your mind on the striking sword even as you see it, and don't keep any thoughts in mind, and meet the oncoming sword directly as soon as you see it, without fixing your mind on it at all, you can take away the sword intended to kill you, and have it turn into a sword to kill your opponent.

In Zen this is called taking the head of the lance and turning it around to stab the other. This means the same thing as taking away the adversary's sword to kill him with what you call "no sword."

Whether the opponent strikes first or you strike first, if you fix your mind on the person at all, or on the sword, the distance, or the timing, your actions will falter. The result will be that you can be killed.

Since your mind is taken up with your opponent when you put yourself in an adversarial position, you shouldn't keep your mind on yourself either.

Reining in your mind to keep it on your body is something to be practiced only as a beginner.

If you set your mind on the sword, your mind is taken up with the sword. If you set your mind on timing, your mind is taken up with timing. If you set your mind on your own sword, your mind is taken up with your own sword. In any case, your mind lingers and your action falters.

Although this was written for a martial artist and therefore uses the appropriate idiom, in the customary Zen manner it naturally extends analogically beyond its overt context. According to Buddhist understanding, the nature of ordinary reality is interactive, not static; so the image of the duel symbolizes the dynamic relationship of the individual to the constantly changing situation presented by the surroundings, especially by the conditions and milieu of one's professional occupation. The "no sword" maneuver, in which an unarmed warrior makes use of an opponent's weapon to snatch victory from defeat, symbolizes the ultimate resourcefulness of the independent Zen adept; it is also a good metaphor for the process of Japan's modernization over the last century.

In his shorter essays "No Gap" and "Mind Like a Spark," Takuan uses Zen terms to explain the way of fluidity in action. He explains spontaneous responsiveness in terms of immediacy, but he does not identify this with speed. It is not quickness of action but immediacy of attention that makes this possible, the Zen master writes, emphasizing freedom of mind.

When you clap your hands a sound comes out immediately, without any interval. The sound does not deliberately come out a while after you clap, it comes right out as you clap.

If your mind stops on the sword your opponent is swinging at you, a gap opens up; and in that gap your action falters.

If there is no gap between your opponent's striking sword and your action, the sword of the adversary will become your sword.

A mind like a spark means the state of mind where there is no gap. When a flint is struck, sparks fly at once. This also means there is no interval for the mind to stop and linger.

It is wrong to understand this only in terms of speed. It means you shouldn't let the mind linger on things, that you shouldn't set the mind on anything, even speed.

If attention lingers, your mind is taken over by others. If you act quickly counting on speed, your mind is also taken over by this attitude.

For centuries there has been a marked tendency in Zen circles to identify speed with spontaneity, due to the use of the former as an imitation or substitute for the latter. It is to this illusion that Zen master Takuan alludes here. The same idea still exists in Zen schools where ritual dialogue is highly prized. It was also fostered in the West by the popular writer D. T. Suzuki, who often gave the impression that Zen depends on quickness of wit, to the degree that any sort of nonsensical statement or action will do as long as it is so rapid as to appear spontaneous.

As a result of this, the distinction is blurred between automatic reactions (such as saying or doing whatever springs to mind at the moment) and the precise awakened response of fluid awareness as originally developed in authentic Zen. D. T. Suzuki's professed belief that Zen enlightenment is irrational also helped to shield this sort of misperception from critical examination within the context of Zen itself as it was known through his writings in the West.

Zen master Takuan, in contrast, points out that the very idea of speed as spontaneity becomes a point of fixation itself. This is amply borne out by Western literature on Zen following the doctrines of D. T. Suzuki. Fascination with quickwitted repartee had already been repudiated by the great Chinese Zen master Dahui five centuries before Takuan, but samurai-oriented Japanese Zen schools seem to have reinstated the cult of speed because of their own concern with the practice of martial arts.

Nevertheless, genuine spontaneity emerging from the immediacy of centered open awareness (rather than from conditioned reflex) is prized not only by Zen warriors, but by all who seek to apply Zen consciousness to actual life situations. In his essay "Where to Set the Mind," Takuan thus proceeds to enumerate the points at which the warrior's mind is unwittingly trained to stop and linger. Finally he shows how the Zen mind transcends these fixations, even the most abstract. This includes a common fixation of Zennists, concentration on one yogic technique that warriors and cultists pursued to great lengths.

Where to set the mind?

If you set your mind on an opponent's actions, you have your mind taken up by the opponent's actions.

If you set your mind on an opponent's sword, you have your mind taken up by the opponent's sword.

If you set your mind on the thought of killing an opponent, you have your mind taken up by the thought of killing the opponent.

If you set your mind on your own sword, you have your mind taken up by your own sword.

If you set your mind on your determination not to be killed, you have your mind taken up by the determination not to be killed.

If you set your mind on people's postures, you have your mind taken up by people's postures.

The point is that there is nowhere at all to set the mind.

Some people say, "If we have the mind go anywhere at all, the mind will be fixated by where it goes, putting us at a disadvantage to adversaries. So put the mind in your gut and keep it there, while adapting to what adversaries do."

Of course, this could be, but from the point of view of an advanced stage of Buddhism, to keep the mind in the lower abdomen is a low stage. It is the stage of practice, the stage of remembrance of seriousness, the stage referred to as "seeking the free mind." It is not the higher transcendental stage, it is the mood of seriousness.

If you force your mind into your gut below your navel and

determine to keep it there, your mind is taken up by the determination to keep it there, so your forward action is deficient and you become extraordinarily unfree.

The now popular practice of settling attention in the lower abdomen (hara) was apparently introduced to Japan around the year 800 C.E. It was part of the meditation lore of the Tendai school of Buddhism, which was established in Japan about that time. In the context of Tendai Buddhism, this exercise is presented as an ancient healing technique. Its immediate efficacy in promoting the power of mental stability (jōriki), however, seems to have been its main source of attraction to martial artists. Although it is now commonly associated with Zen Buddhism (which originally was closely related to the Tendai school) as a means of cultivating concentration (zenjō), there is hardly any notice of it at all in the meditation instructions of the classical Japanese Zen masters.

The practice of concentration in the hara was attributed to Taoist health lore by an eighteenth-century Japanese Zen reviver. He used it to cure some acute nervous and physical problems that he suffered as a result of pondering Zen koans too intensely; among the followers of his school, however, it seems to have become a general method of concentration. The practitioners of this form of Zen will say that they work on koans, or Zen stories, in their gut. Over the last century and a half, this school of Zen acquired great influence among the upper classes in Japan, and the deceptively easy belly-concentration technique passed readily into Western versions of Zen, with virtually no questions asked.

Nevertheless, it was probably through Bushidō rather than pure Zen that this practice spread among the common people of Japan to the degree that expressions such as Hara ga dekite iru ("The gut is accomplished") and Hara ga suwatte iru ("The gut is set") are colloquially used to refer to a calm, collected, imperturbable personality. It can be an image of maturity in general, but it can also apply to serenity and sobriety in face of a particular life-and-death challenge. In either case, the manner of usage is very typical of Bushidō over the last two centuries.

According to the Tao Te Ching, "A way that can be articulated is not a permanent way." In this gut meditation exercise, Zen adopted only a small portion of the more complete tradition of Taoism. Later Zennists and followers of Bushidō in Japan seem inclined to make it into a permanent mind-body posture. Some Chinese Taoists do the same thing, but unlike modern Japanese Zen literature, Chinese Taoist writings abound with warnings about dangers in this practice, especially for women.

Most of these caveats are based on the harm on overdoing things. The premodern reviver of the culturally dominant Rinzai school of Zen took up Taoist techniques to cure some very serious symptoms admittedly caused by overdoing meditation on Zen koans. Taoists also say that their own traditional practices are harmful when overdone. And yet ever since the time of the Rinzai revival there have been Zennists who overdo both koan meditation and belly-attention.

This is not only irrational in itself in Buddhist and Taoist terms, it also makes a person who does it for a long time become irrational. D. T. Suzuki's image of illogical Zen may not have been merely his own understanding of the classics, or his own attempt at the art of the advantage, but also a genuine belief based upon personal observations and experiences of a highly involuted meditation system in early modern Japan.

One of the dangers of focusing attention in the lower abdomen, according to classical and modern Taoist sources, is that the practice produces results easily in the realm of calmness and concentration, but it cannot lead to higher enlightenment. The lure of its ease and comfort seems to be a major reason for the prevalence of fixation on it in popular Zen and Taoist cults.

Concentration without wisdom is one of the endemic ills of Japanese Zen, particularly the forms of Zen under the influence of Confucianism and Bushidō. Takuan is one of the rare Japanese Zen masters to point out the negative potential in this simplistic mind-body posture. Referring to focus in the *hara* as an elementary practice not to be kept up permanently, Takuan said that the more advanced Zen posture of nondwelling not only liberates the mind but likewise the body.

> If you don't put your mind anywhere, it will pervade your whole body fully, spreading through your whole being, so that when you need hands it works your hands, when you need feet it works your feet, when you need eyes it works your eyes. Since it is present wherever you need it, it makes the functions you need possible. If you fix the mind in one place, it will be taken up by that place and thus deficient in function.

If you ruminate, you are taken up by rumination, so you should let go of the mind in the whole body, without leaving any rumination or judgment there, and fulfill the function of each place accurately without stopping and lingering anywhere.

If you put the mind in one place, you become warped. To be warped is to be onesided; to be straight is to reach everywhere. The straight mind, or right mind, means the mind extended throughout the whole body, not sticking to one area or direction.

When the mind is put away in one place, with the result that it is deficient elsewhere, this is called a warped mind. It is the warp that we disdain. Fixation on things is called becoming warped, and is disdained on the Zen Way.

If you don't think of where to put it, the mind pervades the whole being. Placing the mind nowhere, employ your attention to each situation as it happens, according to what opponents do.

Takuan further elaborates on mental freedom and bondage in terms of the traditional ideas of practical Zen psychology. The free fluid mind he is trying to convey to the warrior is now described as the *basic mind* or the *unminding mind*. The fixated mind he tells the warrior to abandon is now called the *errant mind* or the *minding mind*. The Zen master Takuan resumes his previous discussion of physical freedom emerging from mental freedom, to explain specific practical details:

The basic mind is the mind that does not stay in one place but pervades the whole body and whole being. The errant mind is the mind fixed on one spot, brooding over some thing.

When the basic mind congeals and focuses on one point, it becomes the errant mind. Once the basic mind is lost, its various functions become deficient. So the fundamental idea is to try not to lose it.

The basic mind is like water, not remaining anywhere; the errant mind is like ice, with which you cannot wash your hands or head.

If you melt the ice into water, so that it will flow anywhere, then you can wash your hands and feet.

If your mind fixes on one spot and lingers on one thing, it freezes. As a result it cannot be used freely, just as ice cannot be used for washing.

If you melt your mind and use it like a flood throughout the whole body, you send it where you want to and put it to use as you will. This is called the basic mind.

It is not too much to say that recovering the basic mind is given primary importance in Zen. The natural poise of the basic mind was also sought by warriors as a center of balance, from which spontaneous action could emerge without inhibition caused by self-consciousness. In his book on martial arts, the warrior Yagyū Munenori also includes a discussion of the basic mind and the errant mind, following this teaching of Zen master Takuan into more concrete avenues:

> The false mind is passion and selfishness. When the false mind arises, the basic mind is hidden and becomes false consciousness; so nothing but bad things come out.
>
> When we make up falsehoods while saying that there is no falsehood, this is itself the false mind, so its falsehood has already become evident. If the heart is true, people will eventually know, without explanations. The basic mind needs no explanations or excuses.
>
> The false mind is sickness in the basic mind. To get rid of the false mind is called getting rid of sickness. When you get rid of this sickness, you have a healthy mind. This healthy mind is called the basic mind, or the original mind.
>
> If you are in accord with the basic mind, you can become a master of the art of war. This principle also applies to anything you may do.

Zen masters and the martial artists who tried to follow the Zen way typically considered the core mental attitudes of their particular ways to be useful in all activities and all walks of life, as they never tired of repeating. They did not believe that they were ultimately training the mind to conform to arbitrary patterns imposed upon the practitioner, but rather to have available the ability to unfold natural potential for fluid response to the situation at hand. Zen master Takuan also elaborates in terms of the Buddhist definitions of "minding" and "unminding," contrasting attitudes that characterize the so-called "errant" and "basic" minds. He illustrates the difference between "minding" as excess thought and "unminding" as unburdened awareness. Like Suzuki Shōsan in his warning about misunderstanding "no thought," Takuan also explains the distinction between "unminding" in a positive sense as fluidity and freedom, and "mindlessness" in a negative sense as blankness or oblivion.

The minding mind is the same thing as the errant mind. Minding means to mull over one thing, whatever it may be. When you think about something in your mind, judgments and ruminations arise, so this is called the minding mind.

The unminding mind is the same as the basic mind, the mind as it is when not frozen or fixated, without judgments or ruminations. The mind that pervades the whole body and permeates the whole being is called the unminding mind. It is the mind not set anywhere. It is not like stone or wood; unminding mind means the mind that does not stay anywhere.

If you linger, there is something on the mind; if you don't linger, there is nothing on the mind. When you have nothing on your mind, that is called unminding mind.

When this unminding becomes your mind, you do not dwell on anything and do not miss anything. In your body it comes out when a need faces it, to fulfill that need.

The mind that stays fixed in one place doesn't work freely. A wheel turns precisely because it isn't fixed. If it is stuck in one place, it won't turn. The mind won't work either when it is fixed in one place.

If you're thinking about something in your mind, you don't hear what people are saying even as you listen. This is because the mind is staying on what you're thinking about.

When your mind is on the thing you're thinking about, it is onesided. When it is onesided, it does not hear when you listen or see when you look. This is because there is something on your mind, meaning something you are thinking about.

When you have removed whatever that is, your mind is unminding and only works when needed, as needed.

The mind that wishes to get rid of what is on the mind also becomes something on the mind. If you don't think of it, it goes away by itself, and you become unminding spontaneously.

If you always act thus, you will eventually reach that state by yourself some day. If you try to do it right away, you don't get there.

An ancient poem says:

> To think you will not think
> Is also thinking of something;

> Will you resolve not to think
> Even of not thinking?

Takuan extends this principle to all the arts in his explanation of a famous passage from Buddhist scripture, "We should enliven the mind without dwelling on anything." One of the most popular Zen legends tells of the enlightenment of an illiterate woodcutter on hearing this passage. That woodcutter later became the supreme master of Zen in China, his story enshrined as an emblem of the capacities hidden in the ordinary mind. Both the scriptural quotation and the traditional Zen associations are perfect settings for the point that Takuan tries to convey to the warrior.

> "We should enliven the mind without dwelling on anything."
>
> In any kind of occupation, when the thought of doing your work arises, your mind lingers on what you are doing. So this passage means that we should enliven the mind without lingering anywhere.
>
> If the mind is not alive where it is to come alive, your hands don't work; if you're walking, you stop right there. Those who enliven the mind to do specific things yet do not stop and linger in the process are called the experts of the various arts.
>
> From the lingering mind there arises the clinging mind, and repetitious routine existence also begins from here. This lingering mind becomes the bond of life and death.
>
> The point is not to stop there with the consciousness that you are seeing the flowers and foliage even as you see the flowers and foliage.
>
> The ultimate point is not to park the mind in one place, even as you see and hear.

Finally, Takuan clarifies the distinction between "seriousness," mentioned earlier as an elementary practice, and the Zen practice of "not dwelling anywhere." This is a point that often confuses Westerners, because the Japanese generally practice "seriousness" more than they do "nondwelling," and the outsider may easily miss the distinction. Takuan explains:

> When you take seriousness as concentration on oneness or unity of attention, not drifting off, you are still fixing the mind in one place. The essential thing is not to let the mind go to the one you are going to kill, even if that means you are not the first to draw your sword.

The (Neo-Confucian) expression "concentration on oneness, not drifting off" and the (Pure Land Buddhist) expression "single-minded, undisturbed" mean the same thing. However, the mind of "seriousness" is not the ultimate in the context of Buddhism. It is a method of training and practice in controlling the mind and keeping it orderly. When this practice has been built up over the years, your mind goes freely wherever you send it.

The stage of "not dwelling on anything" is the higher, final rank. The mind of "seriousness" is the stage at which you deliberately stop the mind from going elsewhere, thinking that it will become disorderly if you let it go, keeping the mind in check with constant vigilance. This is just a temporary measure, to avoid scattering the mind for the time being. If you are this way all the time, you are inhibited.

From this point of view, followers of Zen or Zen arts who impress others with lifelong dedication to "practice" may actually be the most diligent failures. The signs that the warrior Miyamoto Musashi did not succeed in attaining the deepest level of Zen mostly revolve around this very point. His consuming anguish may have been a ruse, on the other hand, in which case Musashi the educator would appear to have been as master of strategy in the Buddhist way as well as in the way of the warrior.

SCHEMES OF THE SAMURAI

In their study of strategy the Japanese warriors used some of the Zen models, but much of the elaboration of the martial arts went beyond the domain of pure Zen. This is particularly true of many of Musashi's tactics, which are undoubtedly powerful when practiced effectively. His devices often seem to have the gut of Zen without the eye of Zen; but this is not at all unusual even among professional Zennists in Japan.

While Musashi's foremost concern is winning, which he has called the root of the warrior's way, Yagyū Munenori focuses more heavily on the ethical underpinnings of warfare, and goes further to extend practical applications of the strategic thinking of warriors into the domain of political and civil affairs. In his book on family traditions, Yagyū writes:

> When a country is pacified, the consideration given to the selection of officials and the security of the nation is also an art of war. When officials pursue personal interest and thus oppress the common people, this above all is the beginning of the end for a nation. To observe this situation carefully, planning in such a way as to avoid letting the state perish through the self-seeking of officials, is like watching an opponent in a duel to see his move before he makes it.

Whereas Musashi wrote of martial arts in terms of a career in society, and pursued them as a science and a way of life, Yagyū's approach is more ethically oriented. In this the Zen and Taoist influences can be seen. This distinction is not made clearly enough when Bushidō, or the unwritten samurai code, is loosely associated with Zen Buddhism, or when a dueler like Musashi is taken to represent the Zen spirit. In contrast to Musashi's militaristic need to win, Yagyū's sense of moral necessity is more Buddhistic:

It is bias to think that the art of war is just for killing people. It is not to kill people, it is to kill evil. It is a stratagem to give life to many people by killing the evil of one person.

There is an old saying, "Weapons are instruments of ill omen, despised by the Way of Heaven. To use them only when unavoidable is the Way of Heaven."

The reason weapons are instruments of ill omen is that the Way of Heaven is the Way that gives life to beings, so something used for killing is truly an instrument of ill omen. So it means that what contradicts the Way of Heaven is despised.

Nevertheless, it also says that to use arms when unavoidable is also the Way of Heaven. What does this mean? Although flowers blossom and greenery increases in the spring breeze, when the autumn frost comes leaves always drop and trees wither. This is the judgment of nature.

This is because there is logic in striking down something when it is completed. People may take advantage of events to do evil, but when that evil is complete, it is attacked. That is why it is said that using weapons to kill people when unavoidable is also the Way of Heaven.

It may happen that myriad people suffer because of the evil of one man. In such a case, myriad people are saved by killing one man. Would this not be a true example of (the Zen saying) "The sword that kills is the sword that gives life"?

The doctrine of killing one tyrant to save many people from oppression is found in the works of the Confucian philosopher Mencius, in the Buddhist "Scripture of the Great Decease," and in Chinese antecedents of the Tendai school of Buddhism. There is not, however, much emphasis placed on this concept in Japanese thought, even by the samurai who could have used it to rationalize their own profession and historical rise to power over the old aristocracy.

In this Japanese Buddhist political thought differs from that of China, where there were many more Buddhist-inspired uprisings than in Japan. This was probably not so much due to differences between Chinese and Japanese Buddhism as to differences in the political philosophies of the two nations. Whereas in China the legitimacy of revolution against tyranny was clearly defined in native classical philosophy, in Japan the Shintō bias of political thought represented the ruling classes as racially superior to the peasantry, and therefore inviolable in respect to socio-political privileges vis-à-vis the common people.

In this respect, the writing of Yagyū Munenori is distinguished by the dominance of Buddhistic morality over the authoritarian concepts of personal loyalty that Bushidō derived from a combination of Shintō and state Confucianism. Although Yagyū Munenori was a teacher of the Shōgun, his Zen teacher Takuan did not spare him criticism, or admonitions on the perils of his situation. Yagyū in turn showed his Zen spirit in his critical attitude toward the structure and practice of government. His moral basis for military action was not obedience to temporal authority, as was so often the case with samurai warriors. In spite of its setting in the context of hierarchical personal relations characteristic of Japanese governments, or perhaps because of that setting, Yagyū's ethical manifesto is directed toward objective ideas.

> There are treacherous people surrounding rulers, who pretend to be righteous when in the presence of superiors yet have a glare in their eyes when they look at subordinates. Unless these people are bribed, they present the good as bad, so the innocent suffer and the guilty gloat. To see the potential for this happening is even more urgent than to notice a concealed scheme.
>
> The country is the ruler's country, the people are the ruler's people. Those who serve the ruler personally are subjects of the ruler just as are those who serve at a remove. How far apart is their distance? They are like hands and feet in the service of the ruler. Are the feet any different from the hands because they are further away? Since they both feel pain and itch the same, which can be called nearer, which further away?
>
> Therefore people would resent even an honest ruler if those close to the ruler bleed those far away and cause the innocent to suffer.
>
> There are only a few people close to a ruler, perhaps five or ten. The majority of people are remote from the ruler. When many people resent the ruler, they will express their feelings. Now when those close to the ruler have all along been after their own interests and not acting in consideration of the ruler, and therefore serve in such a way that the people resent the ruler, when the time comes those close to the ruler will be the first to set upon him.
>
> This is the doing of those close to him, not the fault of the

ruler himself. It is desirable that the potential for such situations be clearly perceived, and that those distant from the rulership are not excluded from its benefits.

Here Yagyū uses a tactic well known in circumstances where there is no reliable mechanism for questioning rulers effectively. Instead of directing criticism at the ruler, he blames the ruler's advisors for the flaws in government policy and administration. In Japan, the power of the position of rulership is traditionally such that weak individuals may occupy it without their personal weakness actually compromising the authority of the rank itself; it is then that courtiers surrounding the ruler may become the determining force of government while avoiding personal liability by working within the framework of peer consensus in the shadow of an unquestioned authority figure.

So Yagyū indirectly recognizes the limitations on the real power of the ruler as an individual person, but this only intensifies his consciousness of a ruler's need to perceive what is actually happening within and without the circle of his cabinet of advisors. Therefore he stresses the need for enhanced perception not only in strategic combat but even more fundamentally in the strategy of statehood.

> To see potential situations accurately is the art of war.
>
> Not forgetting about disturbance when times are peaceful is the art of war. Seeing the situation of states, knowing when there will be disruption, and healing disturbance before it happens, is also the art of war.

The ideal of seeing events before they happen is pursued so as to be able to deal with them before much effort is needed. This concept comes from ancient Taoism by way of Zen, and is applied to all the individual martial arts as well as all sorts of other things. Because the central concern is perceptive fluidity, one of the classical Zen masters even said, "I don't talk about what you do from day to day, my only concern is that your vision is accurate." Yagyū places similar emphasis on keen perception, and shows how it applies to human interactions, in both war and peace.

> The vanguard of the moment is before an opponent has begun to make a move. This first impulse of movement is the energy, or feeling, held back in the chest. The dynamic of the movement is energy, feeling, or mood. To accurately see an opponent's en-

ergy, feeling, and mood, and to act accordingly in its presence, is called the vanguard of the moment.

The hinge is inside the door. To see the invisible workings hidden inside, and to act upon that, is called the art of war at the vanguard of the moment.

In social and professional relationships, since you are acting as you see situations develop, the attitude is the same as that of the warrior, even when there is no discord. The mindfulness to observe the dynamic of situations even in a group is the art of war.

If you do not see the dynamic of a situation, you may remain too long in company where you don't belong and get into trouble for no reason. When people say things without seeing the states of others, get into arguments, and even forfeit their lives as a result, this is all a matter of the difference between seeing or not seeing the dynamic of a situation and the states of the people involved.

Even to furnish a room so that everything is in the right place is to see the dynamic of a situation, and thus involves something of the mindfulness of the warrior's art.

Yagyū's work is generally more abstract and theoretical than that of Musashi, including his treatment of strategy. Musashi outlines a comparatively large number of specific maneuvers, Yagyū delves more deeply into the philosophy and psychology of strategy. In his discussion of "appearance and intention," a compound word for strategy that literally means "outside and inside" or "surface and interior," Yagyū summarizes what is now considered a hallmark of Japanese transactional behavior:

Appearance and intention are fundamental to the art of war. Appearance and intention mean the strategic use of ploys, the use of falsehood to gain what is real.

Appearance and intention inevitably ensnare people when artfully used, even if people sense that there is an ulterior intention behind the overt appearance. When you set up your ploys and opponents fall for them, then you win by letting them act on your ruse.

As for those who do not fall for a ploy, when you see they won't fall into one trap, you have another set. Then even if opponents haven't fallen for your original ploy, in effect they actually have.

In Buddhism this is called expedient means. Even though the real truth is hidden inside while strategy is employed outwardly, when you are finally led into the real truth, the pretenses now all become real truth.

Yagyū's statement about the relationship between expedients and truth in Buddhism is not really in accord with the scriptural teachings, but it is characteristic of much formal Japanese church Buddhism. The apparent ultimate identification of means and end reflected here underlay the formation of all sorts of cults that carried on ritual observances long after their original meaning had been forgotten.

The monumental *Zongjinglu,* a pan-Buddhist encyclopedia used by early Zen founders in Japan three centuries before Yagyū, explains the classical Buddhist position: "You may follow expedient explanations to the extent that you cling to the provisional, to the detriment of the real. But if you attain the complete immediate teaching, then you understand the real and open up the provisional. If you cling to the provisional, then teaching and perception are divided." From this point of view it is hard to avoid the impression that even warriors who studied Zen like Musashi and Yagyū never got over their attachment to the particular way they followed in ordinary life.

This is not to say that there was necessarily anything sinister in Yagyū's simplistic understanding of Zen Buddhism. The Japanese say *Uso mo hōben* ("Even a lie is an expedient"), but this can be used to refer to any sort of aim or goal, a personal matter without any necessary connection at all to the Buddhist origin or meaning of the idea of expedient means of liberation. Yagyū himself illustrates falsehood becoming true in psychological and ethical terms, using the image of Shintō mystery religion in parallel with the way of the warrior.

In the spirit religion there is what is called the mystery of the spirits. The mystery is kept secret to foster religious faith. When people have faith, they and others benefit from it.

In the warrior's way this is called strategy. Although strategy is falsehood, when the falsehood is used in order to win without hurting people, the falsehood finally becomes true.

The first step of Yagyū's strategy for the warrior is to practice the Zen teaching of nondwelling. It is an ancient observation that fixation of mind makes people vulnerable; the Chinese classic *The Art of War* says, "Attack what they will surely defend." The Zen warrior therefore practices the art of not clinging to anything, so as to avoid being caught by anything, as Yagyū explains, following the teaching of Zen master Takuan.

Spirit is the master of mind. Spirit is within, and employs mind outwardly. The mind also directs energy. Employing energy, mind goes outside in service of spirit. When the mind lingers in one place, efficiency is lost. Therefore it is essential to make sure not to keep the mind on one point.

When a householder sends his servant somewhere on an errand, if the servant stays there and doesn't come back, then he's no longer useful. If your mind lingers on something and doesn't come back to its basic position, then your ability in the art of war slips.

So the practice of not letting the mind stay in one place applies to all endeavors, not only to the art of war.

Yagyū's instructions on balance and spontaneity, interweaving the physical and the psychological, are also influenced by Taoism through Zen. As a result, he subtly achieves the extended metaphorical possibilities characteristic of writings in those traditions.

Steps should not be taken too quickly or too slowly. Steps should be taken in an unruffled, casual manner.

It is bad to go too far or not far enough; take the mean. When you go too quickly, it means you are scared and flustered; when you go too slowly, it means you are timid and frightened.

The desired state is one in which you are not upset at all.

Usually people will blink when something brushes by right in front of their eyes. This is normal, and the fact that you blink your eyes does not mean that you are upset. Also, if something is swung at your eyes two or three more times to startle you, not to blink your eyes at all would actually mean you were upset.

To deliberately hold back spontaneous blinking indicates a much more disturbed mind than blinking does.

The immovable or imperturbable mind is normal. If something comes at your eyes, you blink. This is the state of not being upset. The essential point is just not losing the normal state of mind. To try not to move is to have moved. To move is an immovable principle.

It is good to take steps in a normal manner, and in a normal frame of mind. This is the stage where neither your appearance nor your mind is upset.

Overtly the warrior seems to be talking about a duel, but the expression "to take steps" also means to embark upon any purposeful action. In this sense, the frame of mind in which steps are taken is critical to the whole enterprise. Yagyū goes on to describe the extreme limits of attention demanded by the warrior's strategy by explaining two fundamental code words of his craft: "the first principle" and "the first sword" as used in his art. The ulterior meanings of these terms convey both the mood and the practice of the warrior's way.

"The first principle" is a code word in the art of war. In the general art of war, it means to be independent in every possible way. The important thing is what happens when you are hard-pressed. "The first principle" means that you keep that clearly in mind, pay close attention, and make sure you don't get caught out in a pinch.

"The first sword" is a code word for seeing incipient movement on the part of opponents. The expression "the critical first sword" means that seeing what opponents are trying to do is the "first sword" of supreme ultimate meaning.

Understanding the perception of incipient actions of adversaries as the first sword, understand the weapon that strikes according to what they do as the second sword.

Yagyū also emphasizes the particular point that the enhanced seeing of the "first sword" is not developed by the power of the ordinary eye but by the direct vision of Zen mind as it sees into the heart of things.

To see with the eyes is called perception; to see with the heart and mind is called observation, in the sense of contemplation in the mind.

Conversely, the first line of Yagyū's offensive strategy is also defensive, aimed at canceling out opponents' ability to read his own mind as he would read theirs. As in any sleight of hand, distraction becomes a key to both defensive offense and offensive defense. Again Yagyū turns to Zen terminology for an appropriate metaphor.

In Zen there is something called "beating the grass to scare the snakes." To startle or surprise people a little is a device, like hitting at the snakes in the grass to startle them.

To do something unexpected as a ploy to startle an opponent is also an appearance concealing an ulterior intention, an art of war.

When an opponent is startled and the feeling of opposition is distracted, the opponent will experience a gap in reaction time.

Even simple ordinary gestures are used to distract an opponent's attention.

Throwing down your sword is also an art of war. If you have attained mastery of swordlessness, you will never be without a sword. The opponent's sword is your sword. This is acting at the vanguard of the moment.

This sort of strategy is commonly employed in all sorts of interactions in Japan, and elsewhere in the Orient. It was originally grounded in ancient Taoist and Buddhist teachings as an educational device, and adapted to *the art of the advantage* in the classic book of strategy known as *The Art of War*. Now it is widely diffused, and may occur in any sort of transaction.

Westerners unfamiliar with this strategy often have difficulty discerning the interior from the surface, even mistaking the appearance for the intention. Western seekers of Zen have double trouble in this respect, since they also need to distinguish what are in fact Japanese social devices from what are in effect real Zen devices.

Yagyū's last-mentioned strategy, the mastery of "swordlessness," is perhaps the crowning achievement of the warrior's way, which enables one to apply Zen to ordinary life. In theory, "swordlessness" means the ability to defend oneself without a weapon, implying that one uses an opponent's weapon against him. This is not only a technique of swordsmanship but of debate, negotiation, and other forms of competition as well; here Yagyū is faithful to Zen ideals, distinguishing the technical aspects of the art from the original purpose, in order to establish a reasonable way of differentiating unavoidable necessity from selfish aggression in both attitude and action.

"Swordlessness" doesn't necessarily mean that you have to take the opponent's sword. It also doesn't mean that you make a show of sword-snatching for your reputation. It is the swordless art of not getting killed when you have no sword.

The basic intention is nothing like deliberately setting out to snatch a sword.

It is not a matter of insistently trying to wrest away what is being deliberately kept from your grasp. Not to grasp (the opponent's) attempt to keep hold (of the sword) is also "swordlessness." Someone who is intent on not having (his sword) taken away forgets what he's opposed to and just tries to avoid having (his sword) taken away, so he can't manage to kill anyone.

Swordlessness is not the art of taking another's sword. Its purpose is to use all tools freely. If you are even able to take away another's sword when you are unarmed, and make it your own, then what will not be useful in your hands?

This "swordless" art is what modern Japan used in order to become a major industrial power in one century in spite of its small territory and lack of industrially exploitable resources other than human labor and ingenuity. Whether it is in the personal realm of the individual warrior, or in the public domain of an entire nation or culture, the essence of the swordless art is to make resourcefulness your resource. In his *Book of Five Spheres*, Miyamoto Musashi also makes this transition of outlook from the warrior's way to the universal struggle for survival and excellence:

In the science of the arts of war, it is particularly hard to become a master without being on a straight path and commanding a broad view.

If this science is learned successfully, it won't let you down even if you face twenty or thirty opponents alone.

First, if you work diligently on a straight path, keeping the art of war in mind, you can overcome people with your hands and outsee them as well.

When you practice to the degree that you have become completely adept at using the whole science freely, you can overcome people physically; and when your mind is imbued with this science, you can also overcome people mentally.

When you get to this point, how could there be any way for you to lose to others?

Also, in terms of the art of war on a large scale, you win at finding good people, you win at employing large numbers of people, you win at conducting yourself correctly, you win at governing nations, you win at developing people, you win at performance of social custom.

In any walk of life, what helps you know how to avoid losing to others, how to save yourself and your honor, is the science of the art of war.

While he recognized the universal applications of the warrior's art, as a warrior and strategist himself Musashi focused primarily on the most intense and acute forms of contention and resolution. His fundamental principles derive more from *The Art of War* than they do from Zen Buddhism. In the "Water Scroll" of Musashi's *Book of Five Spheres,* he describes classical warrior's postures of balance that are also rules for maneuvering armies.

Even when you are still, your mind is not still; even when hurried, your mind is not hurried. The mind is not dragged by the body, the body is not dragged by the mind. Pay attention to the mind, not the body. Let there be neither insufficiency nor excess in your mind. Even if superficially weakhearted, be inwardly stronghearted, and don't let others see into your mind.

Following *The Art of War,* the original classic of his field, Musashi emphasizes the importance of knowing opponents and learning how to respond adaptively.

To assess the intelligence and strategy of each individual opponent, to know the opponent's strong and weak tactics, to use the knowledge and virtue of the art of war of find out how to overcome all others, is called mastery of this science.

In the context of the large-scale art of war, to see conditions means to know opponents' ups and downs, to know the hearts of adversaries' followers, to size up the situation, discern the enemy's condition, take in the crucial point that will enable you to use your forces effectively enough to win by the principles of the art of war, and fight with knowledge of your aim.

When you are facing a single opponent, it is also necessary to discern how the adversary operates, perceive the opponent's character, see the person's strengths and weaknesses, do what the enemy doesn't expect, and know the enemy's ups and downs, becoming familiar with their rhythms, thus to preempt them.

If your knowledge is powerful, individual conditions will be evident to you. When you master the art of war, you will find many ways to overcome opponents by accurately assessing their minds. This demands deliberate work.

One of the fundamental means of knowing adversaries is to deliberately put them to the test. Japanese people do this to strangers all the time. If the strangers are Westerners, they may not realize that they are being tested, and may mistake the superficial content of the interaction for the underlying meaning. In actual situations of struggle, it is possible to carry on a testing procedure, wage a battle of attrition, and practice the technique of "swordlessness" all at once. Musashi writes:

> As far as attacks made on you are concerned, let opponents go ahead and do anything useless, while stopping them from doing anything useful. This is essential to the art of war.
>
> Here, if you consciously try to thwart opponents, you're already late. First, while doing whatever you do scientifically, thwart the opponent's very first impulse to try something, thus foiling everything. To manipulate opponents in this way is mastery of the art of war, which comes from practice.

At some point, when the Japanese warrior feels that he has stored enough energy and that his opponent has presented a suitable gap, there may be a sudden conclusion to an interaction. Although obvious in performances of traditional martial arts, when this phenomenon occurs in the context of more complex events it can bewilder or mystify an uninformed onlooker. It would probably be safe to say that all Japanese warriors conscious of their art tried to cultivate this exercise of power, which Musashi describes in characteristically simple terms.

> It is possible to attain certain victory by means of the mood of total absorption of purpose in a single telling blow. The art of war cannot be understood without proper learning. If you can cultivate this sense of the mood of total absorption in a single telling blow, you can master the art of war as a way to win at will.

The power of total concentration has also traditionally been cultivated by Japanese people in other walks of life, often very successfully. In Musashi's case, a consuming personal absorption in the warrior's way and the martial arts clearly led to his unusual elaboration of the science of strategy in conflict.

Musashi's obsession seems to have adversely affected his other relationships—with women, the world, and Zen—but his *Book of*

Five Spheres is in any case ordinarily not read primarily for moral or intellectual values. Whatever Musashi's own intention might have been, the Zen view of this book, as of any other, would be that of the objective observer.

Knowledge of tactics can have defensive as well as aggressive uses. This knowledge can resolve conflict by diffusing it and avoiding it as well as by winning it. From the Zen point of view, one of the arts of this science, as again of any other, is to know when to use it and when not to use it.

This is true of all knowledge, according to the Buddhist concept of *skill in means,* by which is meant the active adaptation of wisdom to situations at hand. It is particularly true of those branches of knowledge dealing with extraordinary powers, such as the art of war.

Miyamoto Musashi's classic of strategy and martial arts may present the greatest need for such caveats, to the extent of its excellence in explaining certain forms of power. His treatment of specific maneuvers is very clear-cut, awaiting only the reader's engagement to translate the abstract principles into understanding of current events.

The following essays from the notorious "Fire Scroll" of Musashi's neo-classic *Book of Five Spheres* are prime examples of the philosophy of winning or "art of the advantage" that distinguishes the warrior's way from Zen Buddhism. These strategies are in themselves amoral from the point of view of the art of war, but to a Buddhist view they are immoral in the service of any cult of win and lose. Perhaps this is why no Zen scholar ever made them more accessible than did Musashi himself.

DISINTEGRATION

Disintegration happens to everything. When a house crumbles, a person crumbles, or an adversary crumbles, they fall apart by getting out of rhythm with the times.

In the art of war on a large scale, it is also essential to find the rhythm of opponents as they come apart, and pursue them so as not to let openings slip by. If you miss the timing of vulnerable moments, there is the likelihood of counterattack.

In the individual art of war it also happens that an adversary will get out of rhythm in combat and start to fall apart. If you let such a chance get by you, the adversary will recover and thwart you. It is essential to follow up firmly on any loss of poise on the part of an adversary, to prevent the opponent from recovering.

MOVING SHADOWS

"Moving shadows" is something you do when you can't discern what adversaries are thinking.

When you can't see your opponent's state, you pretend to make a powerful attack to see what the enemy will do.

ARRESTING SHADOWS

"Arresting shadows" is something you do when adversaries' aggressive intentions toward you are perceptible.

In the art of war on a large scale, this means to arrest the enemy's action at the point of the very impulse to act. If you show the adversaries strongly how you control the advantage, they will change their minds, inhibited by this strength.

You too change your attitude to an empty mind, from which you take the initiative; this is where you win.

In the individual art of war as well, you use an advantageous rhythm to arrest the powerful determination of the adversary's motivation; then you find the winning advantage in the moment of pause, and now take the initiative.

This requires a lot of work.

INFECTION

There is infection in everything. Even sleepiness can be infectious, and yawning can be infectious. There is even the infection of a time.

In the art of war on a large scale, when adversaries are excited and evidently are in a hurry to act, you behave as though you are completely unfazed, giving the appearance of being thoroughly relaxed and at ease. Do this, and adversaries themselves are influenced by this mood, becoming less enthusiastic.

When you think the opponents have "caught" that mood, you empty your own mind and act quickly and firmly, thus to gain the winning advantage.

In the individual art of war as well, it is essential to be relaxed in body and mind, notice the moment an opponent slackens, and quickly take the initiative to win.

ENTRANCING

There is also something called "entrancing" that is similar to "infection." One entrancing mood is boredom. Another is restlessness. Another is faintheartedness. This all takes work to accomplish.

UPSET

"Upset" happens in all sorts of things. One way it happens is through a feeling of being under acute pressure. Another is through a feeling of unreasonable strain. A third is through a feeling of surprise at the unexpected.

In large-scale warfare, it is essential to cause upset. It is critical to attack resolutely where enemies are not expecting it; then while their minds are unsettled, use this to your advantage to take the initiative and win.

In individual combat, you appear relaxed at first, then suddenly charge powerfully; as the opponent's mind changes pitch, it is essential that you follow what he does, not letting him relax for a moment, perceiving the advantage of the moment and discerning right then and there how to win.

FRIGHT

There is fright in all sorts of situations. This is the mind frightened by the unexpected.

If you can seize the moment of fright, you can take advantage of it to win.

STICKING TIGHT

"Sticking tight" means when you are fighting at close range and see that it isn't going well, you then stick tight to the opponent. The essential point is to take advantage of opportunities to win even as you wrestle together.

COMING UP AGAINST CORNERS

"Coming up against corners" means that when you push anything strong, it hardly gives way just like that.

In the art of mass warfare, observe the opposing troops; where they have surged ahead, hit the corner of this strong front, and you should get the advantage.

As the corner collapses, everyone gets the feeling of collapse. Even as they are collapsing, it is essential to realize when each corner is ready to go, and sense when to overcome it.

In the individual art of war also, when you inflict pain on part of his body each time the opponent makes an aggressive move, his body will weaken by degrees until he is ready to collapse and it is easy to beat him.

It is essential to study this carefully to discern where you can win.

FLUSTERING

To fluster opponents means to act in such a way as to prevent them from having a steady mind.

In the mass art of war, it means you assess adversaries' minds on the battlefield, and use the power of your knowledge of the art of war to manipulate their attention, making them think confusing thoughts about what you are going to do; it means finding a rhythm that will fluster adversaries, accurately discerning where you can win.

In the individual art of war also, you try various maneuvers according to the opportunity of the moment, making the opponent think that you are going to do now this, now that, now something else, until you find the opponent starting to get flustered, and thus win at will. This is the essence of battle.

CRUSHING

"Crushing" requires a crushing mood, as when you view an adversary as weak and become strong yourself, thus overwhelming the opponent.

In the art of mass war, this means you look down upon an enemy whose numbers are small; or even if there are many of them, when opponents are demoralized and weakening, you concentrate your force on crushing them, thus mowing them down.

If your "crushing" is weak, it can backfire. You have to carefully distinguish the state of mind in which you are fully in control as you crush.

In the individual art of war also, when your opponent is not as skilled as you are, or when his rhythm is fouled up, or when he starts to back off, it is essential not to let him catch his breath, don't even give him time to blink his eyes; mow him right down.

The most important thing is not to let him recover. This should be studied very carefully.

MOUNTAIN AND SEA CHANGING

"Mountain and sea" means that it is bad to do the same thing over and over again. You may have to repeat something once, but it shouldn't be done a third time.

When you try something on an adversary, if it doesn't work the first time, you won't get any benefit out of rushing to do it again. Change your tactics abruptly, doing something completely different. If that still doesn't work, then try something else.

Thus the science of the art of war involves the presence of mind to "act as the sea when the enemy is like a mountain, and act as a mountain when the enemy is like a sea."

This requires careful reflection.

KNOCKING THE HEART OUT

When you fight with an enemy and appear to win by your skill in this science, the opponent may still have ideas, and while appearing to be beaten still inwardly refuse to acknowledge defeat. "Knocking the heart out" is for such cases.

This means that you suddenly change your attitude to stop the enemy from entertaining any such ideas, so the main thing is to see enemies feel defeated from the bottom of their hearts.

You can knock the heart out of people with weapons, or with your body, or with your mind. It is not to be understood in just one way.

When your enemies have completely lost heart, you don't have to pay attention to them anymore. Otherwise, you remain mindful. If enemies still have ambitions, they will hardly collapse.

BECOMING NEW

When fighting with enemies, if you get to feeling snarled up and are making no progress, you toss your mood away and think in your heart that you are starting everything anew. As you get the rhythm, you discern how to win. This is "becoming new."

Any time you feel tension and friction building between yourself and others, if you change your mind that very moment, you can prevail by a distinctly different advantage. This is "becoming new."

In the art of war on a large scale it is essential to understand "becoming new." It is something that suddenly appears through the power in knowledge of the art of war.

This must be well considered.

SMALL AND LARGE

When you are fighting enemies and get to feel snarled up in petty maneuvers, remember this rule of the art of war: while in the midst of minutiae, suddenly you shift to a large perspective.

Changing to great or small is an intentional part of the science of the art of war. It is essential for warriors to seek this even in the ordinary consciousness of human life.

A COMMANDER KNOWING SOLDIERS

"A commander knowing soldiers" is a method always practiced in times of conflict after having reached the mastery to which one aspires: having attained the power in the knowledge of the art of war, you think of your adversaries as your own soldiers, understanding that you should do with them as you wish, intending to manipulate them freely. You are the commander, the opponents are the troops. This takes work.

BEING LIKE A ROCK WALL

"Being like a rock wall" is when a master of the art of war suddenly becomes like a rock wall, inaccessible to anything at all, immovable.

THE THIRTY-SIX STRATEGIES

Although the works of such Japanese martial artists as Miyamoto Musashi and Yagyū Munenori are readily available in modern Japan, even there the original Chinese tradition of *the art of the advantage* remains unrivaled. One of the ironies of Japanese history is that this art has always been used most successfully in just about every domain besides armed conflict. One might say that the original science itself would predict such an outcome, but it does appear to be paradoxical or ironic when viewed exclusively within the context of Japanese history.

While the Japanese warriors themselves may have been influenced by Zen Buddhism, most of their strategy comes from the Chinese art of war.

The body of this book began with a look at the way of the Japanese warrior as understood by two of its most famous practitioners. Their primary emphasis at the outset is on learning, not as a hobby or intellectual pursuit, but as a way of learning how to live.

For the warrior, above all this means learning how to live well under duress, how to survive chaos. Therefore this book turns to Zen Buddhism, a wellspring of the unassailable inner equanimity that the warrior seeks. Although there is no such distinction in absolute Zen, there are specific teachings for different human types and personalities. Since the warriors were held up to the people of all classes during the centuries of military rule in Japan, certain aspects of the culture of the samurai, including the art of the advantage as well as the Zen teachings specifically directed at warriors, came to exert a pervasive influence in Japanese society.

Because of the extremely long duration of military rule in Japan, the balance in Bushidō between Zen and the art of the advantage seems to have tilted decidedly toward the latter. This would appear to be so much so, in fact, as to have even influenced Zen Buddhism itself into peculiarly Japanese forms heavily marked by elements of the art of war. This book therefore turns from Zen for warriors to the topic of pure strategy.

Whether through traditions of political and military psychology and strategy, or through warrior Zen and the arts it fostered, there is no doubt that the ancient Chinese philosophy and science of war are very much present in the culture and manners of contemporary Japan. One of the most popular classic and still current outlines of the traditional art of the advantage is contained in the famous *Thirty-six Strategies.*

In the manner of a master warrior in the classic tradition of *The Art of War,* the author of the *Thirty-six Strategies* is unknown in spite of the renown of his work. The strategies are encapsulated in mnemonic phrases, many of which passed into proverb and are very widely known and used in the Chinese cultural sphere. Here the strategies are translated and decoded, with brief explanations of their meaning.

1. Sneak across the ocean in broad daylight.

This means to create a front that eventually becomes imbued with an atmosphere or impression of familiarity, within which the strategist may maneuver unseen while all eyes are trained to see obvious familiarities.

2. Surround one state to save another.

When a strong group is about to take over a weaker group, a third part can "have its cake and eat it too," gaining a good reputation by attacking the aggressor in apparent behalf of the defender, and also eventually absorb the weakened defender to boot, without incurring the same opprobrium that would be leveled at outright aggression.

3. Borrow a sword to kill another.

When one side in a conflict is weakening, it may draw its own friends into battle, thus delivering a blow to its enemy while conserving its own strength.

4. Face the weary in a condition of ease.

You force others to expend energy while you preserve yours. You tire opponents out by sending them on wild goose chases, or by making them come to you from far away while you stand your ground.

5. Plunge into a fire to pull off a robbery.

You use others' troubles as opportunities to gain something for yourself.

6. Feint east, strike west.

You spread misleading information about your intentions, or make false suggestions, in order to induce the opponent to concentrate his defenses on one front and thereby leave another front vulnerable to attack.

7. Make something from nothing.

You create a false idea in the mind of the opponent, and fix it in his mind as a reality. In particular, this means that you convey the impression that you have what you do not, to the end that you may appear formidable and thus actually obtain a security that you had not enjoyed before.

8. Cross the pass in the dark.

You set up a false front, then penetrate the opponent's territory on other fronts while they are distracted by your false front.

9. Watch the fire from the opposite bank of the river.

You calmly look on when adversaries experience internal troubles, waiting for them to destroy themselves.

10. Hide a sword in a smile.

You ingratiate yourself with enemies, inducing them to trust you. When you have their confidence, you can move against them in secret.

11. One tree falls for another.

Individual sacrifices may have to made to achieve a greater goal.

12. Take the sheep in hand as you go along.

You take advantage of any opportunity, however small, and avail yourself of any profit, however slight. This comes from the story of a destitute traveler walking on a road. As he went along, he came across a flock of sheep; making his way through them, when he emerged from their midst he had a sheep with him. He behaved so calmly and naturally, as if he had been leading his own sheep to market all along, that the shepherd never noticed him.

13. Beat the grass to startle the snakes.

When opponents are reserved and unfathomable, you create some sort of stir to see how they will react. Yagyū mentions this, and also notes that it is used in Zen. Certain Zen sayings and stories are used primarily to test people and find out what they are like.

14. Borrow a corpse to bring back a spirit.

You don't use what everyone else is using, but use what others aren't using. This can mean reviving something that has dropped out of use through neglect, or finding uses for things that had hitherto been ignored or considered useless.

15. Train a tiger to leave the mountains.

You don't go into the fastness of powerful opponents' territory, but induce them to come out of their stronghold.

16. When you want to take captives, leave them on the loose for a while.

Fleeing enemies may turn again and strike desperately if pursued too hotly. If they are given room to run, on the other hand, they scatter and lose their energy. Then they can be taken captive without further violence.

17. Toss out a glazed tile to draw a jade.

You present something of superficial or apparent worth to induce another party to produce something of real worth.

18. To capture the brigands, capture their king.

When confronted with a massive opposition, you take aim at its central leadership.

19. Take the firewood out from under the pot.

When you cannot handle an adversary in a head-on confrontation, you can still win by undermining the enemy's resources and morale.

20. Stir up the waters to catch fish.

You use confusion to your advantage, to take what you want. It may specifically mean taking advantage of a general or particular loss of direction in order to gather followers from among the uncommitted or disenfranchised.

21. The gold cicada molts its shell.

This means leaving behind false appearances created for strategic purposes. Like the cicada shell, the facade remains intact, but the real action is now elsewhere.

22. Lock the gates to catch the bandits.

You catch invading predators by not letting them get away. You don't let them get back to their homelands with what they can get from you. If they escape, you don't chase them, because you will thereby fall prey to the enemy's plot to wear you down.

23. Make allies at a distance, attack nearby.

When you are more vulnerable to those close by than you are to those far away, you can defend yourself by keeping those around you off balance, in the meantime cutting of their field of maneuver by securing a broader ring of alliances surrounding them.

24. Borrow the right of way to attack the neighbor.

You secure the temporary use of another party's facilities in order to move against a mutual enemy. After having used these facilities to prevail over the enemy, you then turn and use them against the party from whom you borrowed them.

25. Steal a beam to replace a pillar.

You try to recruit top talent from among allies, inducing them to join your concern.

26. Point at one to scold another.

You criticize indirectly, getting your point across without confrontation.

27. Feign ignorance without going crazy.

You pretend to be stupid and ignorant, but avoid talking loosely.

28. Let them climb the roof, then take away the ladder.

You maneuver enemies into a point of no return by baiting them with what look like advantages and opportunities.

29. Make flowers bloom on a tree.

You dazzle and deceive the eyes of opponents by showy displays.

30. Turn the guest into the host.

This is when a business is taken over by one of its own clients or consultants.

31. Scheme with beauties.

This refers to using the charms of women to influence key figures in an adversary organization.

32. Scheme with an empty castle.

You appear weaker than you really are, so that opponents may defeat themselves by one of three reactions to your supposed weakness: they may become conceited and complacent, leading to their downfall; they may become arrogant and aggressive, leading to their destruction; or they may assume you are setting up an ambush, leading them to flee of their own accord.

33. Scheme with double agents.

You compromise insiders of other organizations to get them to work for you.

34. Scheme with self-inflicted wounds.

This a technique particularly for undercover agents: you make yourself look like a victim of your own people, in order to win the sympathy and confidence of enemies.

35. Scheme in continuous circles.

When facing a more powerful enemy, you don't oppose by force, and don't concentrate all your resources on only one avenue of strategy; you keep different plans operating simultaneously in an overall scheme.

36. It is best to run.

When overwhelmed, you don't fight; you surrender, compromise, or flee. Surrender is complete defeat, compromise is half defeat, flight is not defeat. As long as you are not defeated, you have another chance to win.

BUSHIDŌ AND CHRISTIANITY:
ETHICAL CROSSROADS

Two aspects of Japanese culture that have traditionally drawn the unfavorable comment of Westerners in virtually all fields are matters of reason and ethics. A great deal of emotional writing on this subject seems to boil down to the fact that the Japanese have their own reason and morality in addition to what have been borrowed from other cultures.

Those who are unlike the Japanese in their patterns of thinking, believing, and behaving, and who have also been unable to understand the Japanese in these respects, have often written that the Japanese are not reasonable or ethical. Since almost everyone says this about almost everyone else when there are disagreements, this is not in itself a unique phenomenon.

In the case of Japan, what is probably most nearly unique in recent times is the fervor of such denunciations. Writers in this vein, whether in missionary, commercial, or political spheres of operation, will often be found to have a history of unsuccessful attempts to win Japanese people over to what they themselves believe to be reasonable and ethical. As a result, some Japanese have also learned to tell Westerners, when it suits their purposes to do so, that they are by nature not reasonable or ethical people.

It would seem odd that this tactic apparently works like a charm, but it is not so strange when understood in the context of the "art of the advantage," which properly takes place *after* the moral of the situation is determined, and therefore has no ethical content itself beyond the aim of winning for what has been judged right for that time.

There is a great deal of literature touching on this subject, in both Japanese and Western languages. Much of the latter is very recent and quite accessible to the average person. All that can be profitably added here is a summary of the religious roots of Japanese Bushidō and a sampling of the material that is available to the average Japanese today wishing to cultivate those roots. They are not necessarily descriptions of "Japanese culture" in general, but as it may be manifested in particular individuals, organizations, policies, and behaviors.

The Taoist classic *Tao Te Ching* says, "Knowers don't generalize, generalizers don't know." To say that certain ideas or practices are commonly available does not mean that they are actively used in any uniform proportion by the Japanese in general. There are already enormous ranges of quantitative and qualitative differences within each of the root traditions; the same is true of Bushidō and its emanations through Japanese culture. There are many points of contradiction among the root teachings themselves, as well as between religious principles and customary usage.

Then again, philosophical ideas are notoriously subject to varying interpretations and applications, further increasing the breadth of the spectrum of influence that religions can have on societies, far beyond their original purpose. To take generalizations and clichés about Japanese culture at face value, or to take them for their powers of attraction or repulsion, would therefore seem above all to be inviting defeat in the art of the advantage at a very simplistic level indeed.

To be sure, the myths of the difficulty of the Japanese language and the impenetrability of Japanese thinking have contributed most of all to their own authentication. Were even the simplest facts about the language and culture generally known, however, it would be common knowledge not only that these myths can be scientifically disproven, but that their creation and maintenance are among the thirty-six classical strategies outlined in this book.

One might wonder why the West has been so slow to grasp the realities of Japanese thought, in comparison with the well-known alacrity with which the Japanese learned Western ways. It would appear that there were always people who could see both ways, but the mass perceptions of both sides have always been fragmented and exaggerated. The camouflage of mystery and caricature are also part of the art of the advantage, included in the thirty-six strategies; *and it is not only the Japanese who are using them.*

The original roots of Japanese morality are in Shintō, the general term for native religion. Common derivations from Shintō sources are such elements of Japanese culture as cleanliness and other home rituals; belief in spirits, blessings, and curses; sword and other object fetishes; authoritarianism, tribalism, racism, and nationalism. Shinto is not, as commonly claimed, essentially a form of nature worship, although it involves in part the Shintoist's relationship with certain aspects of nature. Some elements of Shintō are very powerful in the modern Japanese subconscious, but no Shintō nature worship has stopped modern Japan from ravaging, pillaging, and polluting nature at home and abroad in the same way that industrialized Christian nations have done.

One of the characteristics of Shinto practice that is commonly noted is its emphasis on benefit in this world. People pray to avert disaster and beckon fortune, whether natural, human, or divine. It is ordinarily said that the Japanese aristocracy took to Tantric Buddhism so readily because its accommodation of this element allowed it to assimilate Shintō easily. The early Zen masters tried to break away from this materialistic orientation in Japanese religion, but an outstanding Zen teacher of the fourteenth century was still complaining that Zen was being ruined by demands that the monks say prayers for the success and welfare of their samurai patrons.

The first Zen master in Japan to write extensively on good and evil was Dōgen Zenji (1200–1253), a prolific author and one of the Zen teachers consulted by Hōjō Tokiyori, distinguished regent of the first central Shogunate. Dōgen was one of the most adamant of those who rejected the widespread use of Buddhism for social, political, and material power; and he was driven out of the capital area for his trouble. In his essay "Don't Do Any Evil," one of the ninety-five chapters of his magnum opus *Shōbōgenzō*, Dōgen wrote on the relativity of conventional morality:

> There are sameness and differences between evils in this realm and evils in other realms; there are sameness and differences between prior times and later times.

Christian thinking tends to absolutize particular frameworks of good and evil as laws of God; Buddhist thinking deals with the relativity of good and evil. This is believed to be one reason for the flexibility of Japanese morality as it is applied in life situations, as compared with Western conceptions of ethics rooted in Christian dogma.

As a Buddhist, Dōgen writes that good and evil are a matter of conditions, including the time, place, and people concerned. According to this philosophy, good and evil depend on context as a whole, their existence and specific characteristics relative to the individual differences in subjective and objective experiences therein. Therefore while Zen master Dōgen wrote extensively on ethics for his time, the central principle of relativity stands out in his metaphysical work on the roots of morality. His greatest philosophical achievement in this domain was undoubtedly in his representation of the total context of human behavior in the light of Flower Ornament Buddhism. One of the most poignant examples of this is found in the *Shōbōgenzō* essay entitled "The Whole Works":

> Life is like when you ride in a boat: although in this boat you work the sail, the rudder, and the pole, still the boat carries you, and you are nothing without the boat. Riding in the boat, you even cause the boat to be a boat.
>
> You should contemplate this precise point. At this very moment, the boat is the world. Even the sky, the water, and the shore have all become circumstances of the boat, unlike circumstances that are not the boat.
>
> For this reason, life is our causing to live; it is life's causing us to be ourselves.
>
> When riding in a boat, the mind and body, object and subject, are all workings of the boat. The whole earth and all of space are both workings of the boat. We that are life, life that is we, are the same way.

While it has historically been at least as difficult for the Japanese to sustain this perspective on a global scale as it has been for other highly self-conscious civilizations, still parallel if less profound and universal concepts of ethical relativity, restraint, and communal interdependence are part of everyday life in Japan. One of the avowed aims for education in post-industrial Japan is to produce the "international person," applying the original Buddhist concept to the needs of the contemporary world.

A sourcebook of Japanese thought more popular than any Zen text may be found in the work known as *Tsurezuregusa,* in which the familiar roots of ordinary Japanese feelings are clearly exposed. Full of Buddhist, Confucian, and Taoist ideas as well as native Japanese ideas, this book is part of a normal Japanese language curriculum and therefore has far wider currency today than any classic scripture or sectarian religious work. Sometimes it directly reflects Japanese ideas and practices that are presently very familiar throughout the modern world; sometimes in voicing Taoist, Buddhist, or Confucian beliefs it is highly critical of customary usage. Because of the literary and exoteric nature of the work, the writer's viewpoint is more easily observed than is the case in classic Zen writings.

As is well known, the family is a traditional seat of civilization and its institutions in the Orient. It is within the family that the individual is originally schooled in the feelings that are to be the individual's bond to society, and that have become the cement of the society itself. Whereas the Christian recites the precept "Honor your father and mother" as a commandment of the supreme God, the Japanese understands familial feelings as a rational duty inherent in the nature of society. The author of *Tsurezuregusa* illustrates this sense of intimate connection between family life and the condition of society as a whole:

> Even people who seem to be ignorant do sometimes say good things. Once a fearsome warrior from the borderlands asked one of his companions, "Do you have any children?" The other man replied that he had none. The first warrior said, "Then you don't understand life. You must be awfully cold. Only when you have children do you fully understand life."
>
> This is certainly true. If not for human love, how could there be compassion in the heart of anyone like this warrior? Even people without any sense of duty towards their parents will come to know how their parents felt once they themselves have children.
>
> People who retire from society to become hermits free from mundane cares are wrong to look down on people with worldly ties and desires who cultivate social relations. If you consider the matter from the point of view of people with worldly ties, it is truly pitiful—for the sake of their parents, spouses, and children, they even forget about shame, and may even have to steal.
>
> So rather than arresting thieves and just punishing crimes, it would be preferable to run society in such a way that people do not go hungry and cold.
>
> When people lack a constant means of livelihood, they lack psychological stability. When they are desperate, people steal. When society is not functioning properly and people are cold and hungry, there can be no end to crime.

Many of the moral teachings whose traces remain imprinted on Japanese feelings in various proportions deal with relationships and attitudes rather than with isolated acts in themselves. The author of

Tsurezuregusa highlights the emotional source of moral sense, concluding that the recognition of human feeling needs to be incorporated into the logical structure of an argument for rational social organization.

In contemporary Japan a great deal of thought is given to extenuating circumstances in criminal cases. When judgment is impaired by alcohol consumption, for example, or by extreme despair, this is taken into consideration as a real factor in the course of events. Therefore in spite of strict laws and measures, the Japanese criminal justice system does display a certain degree of the human understanding reflected in classic writings.

Some of the social criticism in *Tsurezuregusa* also rings as true today as it did when it was written centuries ago. One of the apparent paradoxes of Japanese society is that whereas almost all the Japanese say that they think of themselves as belonging to the middle class, there is nevertheless a pervasive and compulsive status consciousness. This can become so intense as to become almost unbearably stifling even to those who willingly uphold it. Although this may be considered a relic of former times, its existence and consequences are very real. *Tsurezuregusa* approaches this problem by illustrating the superficiality of the concern for social status as compared with the original values on which it is grafted.

> It is desirable to leave an undying reputation to posterity, but even if people have high rank and status, that doesn't necessarily mean they are superior people. Even fools and incompetents can rise to high office and live luxuriously if they are born in the right families and have good luck. There have been many fine people with virtue and wisdom who were of lowly status and never had much of a chance in life.
>
> Obsessive concern for high office is nearly as stupid as obsessive desire for material wealth. While it is desirable to leave behind a distinguished reputation for wisdom and heart, yet on careful examination one will find that a liking for good repute is enjoyment of fame. But neither those who praise nor those who criticize remain in the world, and those who will hear such reports also soon pass away. So whose opinions of you should you be concerned about?
>
> Praise, furthermore, is at the root of criticism. There is no benefit in leaving a name after death. So to wish for fame is nearly as stupid as wishing for high status.

In contrast to the pretensions of ambitious Japanese aristocrats and warriors (which were generally much like those of aristocrats and warriors everywhere), one of the virtues for which the common Japanese people are often praised is the quality of modesty. This has its roots in mystical Shintō, where the simple and honest heart becomes the sacred lodging of the spirit. It is more intellectually refined in Buddhism, where it is a psychological device, a means of streamlining the individual's passage through life. Certain passages of *Tsurezuregusa* underline the foundations of modesty from a point of view that combines feeling and reason, including the simplicity of the Taoist and the sophistication of the Buddhist.

> It is best not to pretend to know all about everything. Even if they do know something, cultivated people do not advertise the fact. It is the bumpkin who talks as though he knows everything. Even if one is outstanding in some way, to think of oneself as impressive is unbecoming. It is better not to talk much about what one knows, not to speak of it unless asked.
>
> When ignorant people make assessments of others and think that they know what others know, they cannot be right. For example, when someone who lacks intelligence but is good at chess sees intelligent people who are not good at chess, he thinks they are not as smart as he is. And when he sees people who are skilled at all sorts of arts but don't know how to play chess, he thinks he is better than they are. This is a big mistake.

Earlier, in the discussion of the way of the Zen warrior, it was noted that the attitude of seriousness is one of the psychological exercises of Neo-Confucianism, an educational system that exerted tremendous influence on the Japanese mind over centuries of orthodoxy under samurai rule. This mental set has come to form one of the bases of a certain Japanese moral feeling, according to which a person is judged less by the content of the undertaking than by the mood of seriousness, the depth of devotion and concentration brought to bear on the action. Again *Tsurezuregusa* reflects on the rationale underpinning the absorption in this mood of which the Japanese are so remarkably capable.

> In any field of endeavor, specialists are superior to dilettantes, even if the specialists are not as talented as the dilettantes. This

is because specialists always take their art seriously, while dilettantes are mere hobbyists.

This does not apply only to arts. In all actions and attitudes,
success is based on singleminded seriousness, while failure is
based on whimsicality.

A logical extension of this attitude applied in practical situations
spawned what is now referred to as TQC, or Total Quality Control,
one of the distinguishing features of excellence in Japanese manufac-
turing. *Tsurezuregusa* illustrates the reasoning behind TQC through
a representative scenario in learning to perfect the performance of an
art:

> Once someone learning archery faced the target holding two
> arrows. The teacher said, "Beginners shouldn't hold two arrows,
> because counting on the second arrow results in carelessness with
> the first. Each time, determine that you will settle the matter
> with this one arrow, without worry about whether or not you
> will succeed."
>
> With only two arrows, and in the presence of the teacher,
> would one really be careless with an arrow? You may not be aware
> of any slackening in your own mind, but a teacher will know.
>
> This admonition should be applied to everything. When
> people practice an art, they always think they will have another
> chance to try again, so they are not aware of slackness in their
> minds at the moment. It is very difficult to work in the immediacy
> of the present moment.

Although there are many individual aspects of Japanese civilization
whose classical roots and historical development are relatively clear
and straightforward, as a whole the actual conditions of contemporary Japanese psychology and culture are very complex motleys, since
each element therein has its own history of usage; usually quite long
and already complicated by centuries of changes in relevance and
application to the life of the society and its individual members.

One of the touchiest ethical issues in the context of the encounter
between Japanese Bushidō and Western Christianity is the subject of
killing. It is well known that taking life is expressly forbidden in
Buddhism, just as in Christianity, with the only difference that Buddhism extends its sanction further into the neighboring realms of life
than does the more anthropocentric religion of Christianity.

There is, nevertheless, scripturally based rationale for killing in Buddhism, Taoism, and Confucianism, as when a malicious tyrant is assassinated to save the lives of multitudes. Christianity also has its own version of holy war, although the details of its reasoning may not be quite the same in view of its particular theological background. In Tantric Buddhism there are even spells specifically designed for doing away with evil despots; some translators cut them out of the Chinese versions during the Tang dynasty, but the Japanese Tantrists got hold of them anyway, and they are seldom associated with justice. Although the only Buddhist-led wars in old Japan were popular uprisings and self-defense operations, to this day it is the image of wicked barons with devilish Tantric assassins in their employ that is in the popular mind's eye through television drama.

In the twelfth and thirteenth centuries there were a number of major reform movements among Japanese Buddhists. This was when such well-known schools as Zen, Shinshū, and Nichiren arose. One of the outstanding characteristics of early Zen and Shinshū was their rejection of the materialistic inclination that Buddhism had gotten from Shintō. The fourteenth-century National Teacher Musō Soseki, one of the most celebrated Zen Buddhists of all time, was perhaps the most forthcoming in his criticism of prayer for profit. Advisor to one of the co-founders of the second Shogunate, Musō also disallowed the use of justification as a substitute for justice in applying the principle of righteous war; in his famous *Muchū Mondō,* still one of the most accessible classics of Zen, Muso tells the Shōgun's brother:

> The fact that you are now looked up to by a multitude as a military leader is entirely the result of past virtues. Nevertheless, there are still people who oppose you, and few of your vassals follow your direction selflessly. When I see this, it seems to me that there was still some lack in the good causes in your past. So how can it be said that you are doing too many good deeds now?
>
> If you compare your criminal deeds with your virtues, which do you think are more? And how many people have you destroyed as enemies? Where are their surviving families and dependents to go? And not only the deaths of enemies, but also the deaths of your allies in war are all your sins too.

If nothing else, one has to admire Musō's courage in speaking to a warrior in this manner, let alone the brother of the Shōgun himself. National Teacher or not, he had no guarantee whatsoever that the displeasure of the Shogunate would not result directly or indirectly in his death or banishment. According to the Buddhist *Flower Ornament Scripture,* one of the main classical sources of Zen, this is a characteristic type of courage that emerges in the stage of enlightenment known as Intense Joy.

Evidently there were military and political advisors who were unhappy with the new government's pious and charitable works. This is not an unusual theme in Asian politics. Other famous warriors and empire builders in India and China are well known for becoming zealous Buddhists to atone for their sins after bloody wars of conquest, with mixed results.

A similar phenomenon still occurs in the domain of corporate warfare and other forms of competition and conflict. In the realm of international politics and economics as well, recent increases in Japanese foreign aid are publicly interpreted in parallel ethical terms.

Perhaps no phenomenon more distinctly marks the ideological gap between Japan and the West than does the fact that an extremely small number of Japanese have been converted to Christianity in spite of more then a century of missionary work. Had the Shōguns not turned against Christianity and suppressed it in the late sixteenth and early seventeenth centuries, the story might have been very different.

Once they realized that European political and economic ambitions came with the Christian missions, however, the Shōguns seemed to feel that they had no choice at that point but to reject Western overtures. Among the most unusual and informative documents of this process is a tract written by Suzuki Shōsan at the behest of the Shōgun to refute Christian doctrine in the wake of a violently crushed insurrection by Japanese Christians.

This remarkable treatise, which is actually a good deal more intelligent than many anti-Western writings, is not mere polemic, and is no more severe than Suzuki's critique of the decadent Buddhism of his time. It reflects astonishment at the slightness of Christian doctrine in comparison with the vastness of Buddhist thought, reflects wonder at the impudence and bigotry of the missionaries, and decries what is perceived as both mental and material imperialism. As one of the earliest writings on premodern Japanese foreign relations, it is of inestimable value as a political document as well as religious tract; several of the essays are translated below, being of particularly great interest for what they reflect of how the Portuguese and the Japanese perceived one another, as well as for their illustration of a Japanese response to foreign pressure.

1. According to what I hear of the Christian teaching, there is a great Buddha called Deus, who is the one sole Buddha, master of the universe and lord over all. This is the creator of the universe and all beings. This Buddha came into the world in some foreign land to save people sixteen hundred years ago. His name was Jesus Christ. Ignorant of this, they say, other countries honor the worthless Amida Buddha and Gautama Buddha, the height of folly.

Refutation: If Deus, as the master of the universe, created all lands and all beings, why has that Deus hitherto neglected countless nations, not appearing among them?

Ever since heaven and earth were opened, the buddhas of past, present, and future have emerged over and over again to liberate beings. How many hundred of millions of years would you say this has been going on? What basis of proof is there for saying that Deus never appeared in other countries all that time, and only recently appeared in such-and-such a country?

If Deus is the master of the universe, he is sure doing a slipshod job of it if he lets a multitude of the nations he has created be taken over by subsidiary buddhas, suffering them to spread their teachings to liberate beings, ever since the opening of heaven and earth. This Deus is indeed a foolish buddha.

Furthermore, they say that Jesus Christ came into the world and was crucified by ordinary men of the lower world. This is the master of the universe? How could anything be so illogical?

The Christians do not know the unified enlightened state of the true likeness of original awareness. In their ignorance they have taken over one buddha to worship. Their fault in coming to this country to spread devilish teachings and false principles cannot avoid the punishment of Heaven.

There are many ignorant people who cannot understand such simple logic, and throw their lives away out of reverence for that teaching. Is this not a national disgrace? One hardly dare mention what this does to our international reputation.

Although Buddhism is now sometimes referred to as a Japanese religion, it is really transnational at heart. A notable difference between Japanese Buddhism and European Christianity is that the former does not have the same emotional tie to the life of the historical Buddha that the latter has to the birth of Christ. In Mahayana Buddhism, the appearance of a living buddha is not considered a unique historical event as the appearance of Christ was by Church Christians; but rather an infinite, omnipresent possibility that is acted out according to conditions. A buddha was regarded as a reflection, or a reflector, of eternal truths to which all could aspire. The attitude of Zen Buddhism in particular was summarized in a classical statement by a Chinese master to the effect that he studied from the same source as the buddhas.

One point of historical resemblance between Buddhism and Christianity was their break with the tribalism of their original host cultures, Hinduism and Judaism. No longer tied to family and nation, Buddhism and Christianity did anciently share a universal outlook that transcended racial, national, and cultural identity. This having been said, however, it must be added that the habit of self-making is so strong everywhere that new forms of pseudo-tribalism did in fact emerge in both Japanese Buddhism and European Christianity, centered around their various patriarchs, evangels, churches, schools, and sects.

At the time when Suzuki Shōsan wrote his anti-Christian tract, the pseudo-tribal elements in both Buddhism and Christianity were especially strong because of their connection with political, economic, and territorial facts of life. The Christian missionaries were suspected of fronting for European colonial interests; and even those who were only involved in spreading the Gospel were not interested in learning anything about Buddhism that did not serve their own purpose. The Japanese military government did not want a lot of foreign influences or agencies to operate on Japanese soil, certainly not on their own and at their own pace.

The Buddhists, for their part, generally enjoyed cordial relations among a wide variety of sects, including those affiliated with Shintō. Some of these churches used doctrines and practices as diverse in respect to externals as the most dissimilar varieties of even Buddhism and Christianity; yet the Buddhist concept of expediency was sufficient rationale to accommodate them all. They were therefore aghast at the aggressiveness and dogmatism of the European Christian missionaries, especially considering the fact that what appeared to be their doctrine—one local god claiming to rule the world—seemed very slight indeed to the Mahayana Buddhists.

That is not to say that the Jesuits did not have bigger intellectual guns than those they used to convert outcastes, peasants, and merchants. They generally seemed to regard the Japanese as heathens still in the middle ages at the beginning of the seventeenth century, however, with whom there would be no point in discussing the Summa Theologica. Their own knowledge of Buddhism would not in any case have sufficed for the purpose of "matching meanings" with Japanese Zen masters. Over all, the intellectual and political aspects of the relationship between the cultures paralleled each other closely in the subjective and objective experience of both sides.

For the Japanese leadership, it was enough to sense that here were people no better than anyone else coming around with some story about how the Japanese should let Europe take over in the name of Deus, their god who was also no better than anyone else's god. The umbrage felt by the Japanese side was similar to that felt by other nations later when the Japanese Shintō militarists told them they should let Japan oversee their affairs, and also to that felt by yet others when the militaristic Shintoists declared the Japanese destiny of world leadership received by direct inheritance from the Sun Goddess, who was now elevated to the status of a supreme deity.

In the transcultural Buddhist view, this is no way to get along. Although his patriotic duty is to refute the Christian doctrine, Shōsan consistently uses this assignment as an opportunity to teach something about Buddhism as well. From his comparison of the supranational grandeur of Buddhist salvationism with the globally politicized missionary front of Christianity, Shōsan turns to the inconceivable subtlety of the unspoken teaching of Zen in contrast to the doctrinaire line of the Christians. First the cosmic concepts of Mahayana Buddhism and Christianity were compared; now the very psychology of dogmatism itself is exposed to the Zen razor.

2. The fundamental intention of past, present, and future buddhas' appearance in the world is to guide beings directly to enlightenment. Therefore it is said they "point directly to people's mind, so they see its essence and attain awakening."

When Gautama Buddha came into the world, after the

accumulated effects of twelve years of difficult and painful practices had built up, on the eighth day of the last month of the year he realized the design of the true characteristics of all things on seeing the morning star. After that he left the mountains.

Later, when Buddha had finished the discourses on which the scriptures are based, Buddha held up a flower to show to those who had assembled. Now everyone was silent. Only the saint Kasyapa smiled. The Buddha said, "I have a treasury of eyes of truth, and the subtle mind of nirvana. Real characteristics are indefinable; subtle teachings do not stand on words, but are separately transmitted outside of doctrine. This I entrust to Kasyapa."

This was transmitted from Kasyapa to successor after successor, finally coming to Japan, where the principle of communicating mind by mind is still preserved.

What the Christians teach, on the other hand, is focused solely on a view of the reality of existence, which increases thoughts, worries, and conscious emotions, leading them to make up a "creator of the universe," thus reinforcing the habits that make them revolve in mundane routines, while believing this to be the way of enlightenment.

For them to come to this country and try to oppose authentic teachings with such stupid ideas and interpretations is like a sparrow challenging a roc on wingspread, or a firefly telling the moon about light.

This essay begins with the traditional Zen myth of the founding of the extradimensional communication of Zen by Buddha and one of his chief disciples, the saint Kasyapa the Elder. The tale illustrates the Buddhist teaching that formulations of doctrine are provisional expedients designed to provoke special perceptions, not to be elevated to the status of absolute truths. Everyone is aware that purely subjective impressions and feelings cannot be exactly conveyed in words; Zen teaching takes this to the limit by insisting that the experience of the clarified mind cannot be understood just by descriptions of procedures or results, but must be verified in direct experience.

While this is most strongly emphasized in Zen as represented by the unspoken teaching, it is not really peculiar to Zen but is part of Buddhist scriptural tradition. The reason it was stressed by Zen teachers was to counter psychological and political attachments to the externals of dogma and belief, fixations that veiled their victims from the underlying meaning of forms and recreated feelings that ran directly counter to the original purpose of Buddhism. Religion became politicized through these feelings, since sectarian strife could not exist without the connection of proprietary and territorial interests with items of dogma, belief, and ritual.

In contrast to formal transmission of doctrine, Zen emphasized "mind-to-mind" communication of the ineffable. This does not mean something like mental telepathy, however, as it is ordinarily imagined. In early Chinese Zen lore the mind-to-mind acknowledgment is likened to two mirrors reflecting each other with no image interposed. There is also a classical Zen device known as the meeting of minds in a specific realm, which could be abstract or concrete and was often represented overtly only by a symbol, but this practice eventually drifted into the same involutionary pattern as doctrinaire approaches.

The term "transmission of mind by mind" *(i shin den shin)* eventually passed into popular usage in Japan through the spread of Zen, and came to be used in the various arts to refer to an extra element outside the formal structures that only comes to awareness and life through conscious experience. It may also at times be used more vulgarly to describe coincidences of perception or thought that appear to be more precise than what common habit might predict. The original Zen meaning, however, is something very precise and clear, the communication of Zen mind-to-mind by objective experience.

The Christian attitude to which the Zen master objects here is the fixation on assumptions about the reality of existence, not only as the content of dogma but as the motive force of dogmatic thinking. Buddhist metaphysics is more complicated than a simple distinction between existence and nonexistence, or between reality and unreality, so it is not that Shōsan just opposes Christian realism on philosophical grounds alone. Buddhism deals with the psychological consequences of metaphysical concepts as life attitudes, and the critique of the naive realism of the materialistic mind in Europe presented here by Shōsan is not only peculiarly anti-Christian but also traditionally directed at other Asian philosophies, such as Confucianism.

Ironically, Shōsan's explanation of the impulse to "create a Creator" as a means of managing the worries engendered by this bent of mind is fundamentally much the same as that used by one of the most eminent promoters of Christianity in the twentieth century, the Swiss psychoanalyst Carl Jung. Although he proclaimed his opposition to presumptuous authoritarianism in religion, however, Jung did not draw from his psychological argument the conclusion that metaphysical assumptions could be changed as readily as could the psychic facts habitually associated with them.

Zen master Shōsan, in contrast, draws attention to the disparity in depth between the open mind of Buddhist illuminism and the closed mind of missionary Christian dogmatism. The metaphors of the sparrow and the roc, and of the firefly and the moon, are ancient Taoist images used to criticize the mundane, materialistic Confucian political philosophers with their fixed system of rationalizations. The Taoists had much broader perspectives on life than the more rigid and self-righteous Confucians. Metaphysically as well as psychologically, the Taoists believed that being comes from nonbeing, while the Confucians believed in preexisting being. Thus the Zen Buddhists, who were heirs of Taoist thought, could easily see the same patterns in their intellectual and spiritual relationship to doctrinaire missionary Christianity.

The next essay also uses traditional Buddhist rationales, but this time it is in defense of native Japanese religion.

3. I hear they say it is wrong to honor the spirits (kami), and that we only do it because we don't know Deus.

Refutation: Japan is spirit country. Having been born in spirit country, not to honor the spirit luminescences would be the ultimate impropriety.

It is said that the harmonization of spirit with matter begins the formation of affinity, while the complete attainment of enlightenment in all respects consummates the salvation of beings. Therefore the earlier appearance (of buddhas) as spirits, thus making an impact on this country, was an expedient to soften people's hearts and introduce them to the real Way.

The only difference between spirits and Buddha is that between waves and water. The unified enlightened state of the true likeness of fundamental awakeness appears temporally according to people's minds to liberate them. Therefore the attitude of respect for the spirits is also a gesture of gratitude toward that unified enlightened state.

For example, when you respect the ruler of a nation, it is an established principle that you respect everyone in the whole hierarchy of government and society. This is all out of respect for the one person on top. Do not the Christians in effect teach that it is right for those who respect the top man to have no use for anyone below him?

The early Japanese Buddhist giant and culture hero Kūkai had fostered the idea that the native deities were local reflections of more cosmic truths that were now represented by buddhas. The deities were absorbed into Buddhism as helpers, guardians, or even enlightening beings, manifestations of cosmic principles in action. This idea is well developed in the Flower Ornament *(Kegon)* scripture that Kūkai brought to Japan from China. The same syncretic device was also used by Buddhism in other cultures throughout old Asia.

Here Shōsan gives the psychological interpretation, as Zennists usually did, explaining the significance of the deities in terms of the effect their belief exerted in the minds of believers. The essay is then brought to a sudden close on the abrupt note of the immediate crisis, in which a metaphor nearly assumes the status of the main topic.

In Shōsan's essay, the central experience of Buddhist enlightenment and the attitude of reverent attention to a higher thought are symbolized in Shintō-Confucian garb, as was customary for political encounters, and represented as a social order and its seat of power. This point may be incomprehensible to Christians thinking in theological rather than political terms, but Shōsan suggests that logical extension of the monotheism preached by the missionaries would subvert the Japanese social order, because it absolutizes one source of authority without recognizing any intermediary. This spelled chaos to the mind accustomed to hierarchy; Shōsan was undoubtedly not aware that the Christians had their own cults of saints and evangels, with their own corresponding ideas and institutions of kings and aristocracies claiming divine rights.

The next essay is also Shintoistic, extending the idea of deity into the natural world. The influence of Taoism through Neo-Confucianism and Zen is also evident. The Shintō relationship of humanity to the environment is through a feeling of gratitude *to* the world of energy and matter as much as *for* it; the Western Christian relationship is based more completely on a kind of gratitude *for* the material world, not *to* it.

In consequence of the onesidedness of the Christian mode of gratitude, the Westerner suffered no problem of conscience with the idea of maximum exploitation of nature until the damage done thereby had become so great as to be threatening and thus reactivate the primary instinct of life, the very sense upon which the abstract spiritual essence of Shintō is originally based. Although he encountered the vanguard of Western technological advance in a relatively primitive form, Shōsan already sensed a contradiction in the rationale of its moral feeling.

4. I hear they say that the Japanese reverence for the sun and moon is wrong; that these are lamps for the world, and that our reverence is also because of not knowing Deus.

Refutation: The human body is composed of a combination of elements based on passive and active energy. The sun is the embodiment of active energy, the moon is the embodiment of passive energy. How can the body be maintained without the passive and active energies? Since they are our roots, we cannot honor them enough. If you think passive and active energies are worthless, then don't use water or fire.

The blessings of the sun and moon in the sky lighting up the world can hardly be requited. People have two eyes that shed light on them; are they not imbued with the virtues of the sun and moon? Since they say it is meaningless to honor the sun and moon, will the Christians then keep their eyes closed? Such is their ignorance of correct reasoning. This is truly idiotic.

Under the pressure of Western materialism, Japanese industry also became damaging and destructive to the local and global environment, thus to this extent losing the meaning of Shintō as expressed in this essay. For that very reason, the rationalized Shintō of the Zen master Shōsan, simple and naive as it seems, has no less profound a meaning for the future of world culture today than it did when this tract was written in the seventeenth century, when Western Europe was just opening up the Pandora's box of advanced industrial technology placed in the hands of men who no longer believed that the natural world was imbued with spirits to be respected and thanked. The ancient pagan world was now inhabited only by inanimate matter and force, to be processed and sold in the most lucrative manner available.

Rationalism and technological advance were popularly associated with Christianity in Westernizing nineteenth-century Japan when political relations and missionary activity resumed after the dissolution of the feudal Shogunate, but the Christianity presented to the Japanese public of the seventeenth century made more liberal use of supernatural rather than mechanical miracle stories.

It may have been that the Jesuits imagined that the Shintoistic side of the Japanese psyche would be interested in this sort of thing, but at least in Shōsan's hands the presence of many similar stories in native Japanese traditions redounds against this missionary Christianity. Buddhism had long before relegated the supernatural to the status of relative truth, and did not attribute to it the imagined connection to absolute truth projected by the mind of the naive realist confronted with the inexplicable but undeniable. In response to Christian tales of miracles, Shōsan writes:

5. I have heard that Christians generally honor marvelous things and attribute them to the glory of Deus. They fabricate all kinds of ruses to fool people.

If marvels were valuable, then the king of deceivers should be revered. Foxes and badgers in this country also work marvels.

It is said that when the god Indra fought with the king of the titans, the titan was defeated and led his 84,000 followers into the hole of a lotus fiber to hide. Do you also honor this kind of marvel?

The six psychic powers are clairvoyance, clairaudience, communication with other minds, awareness of past lives, psychic flight, and knowledge of the end of psychological leakage. The first five of these powers are also found in masters of mesmerism and unliberated religions. The power of knowledge of the end of psychological leakage, however, is beyond mesmerism and unliberated religion; it is the awakened knowledge where all psychological afflictions have been ended.

Therefore there is nothing marvelous about the six powers of a buddha. That is why it is said that there are no marvels in Buddhism. Those who do not know this principle can be fooled by mesmerism and unliberated religion.

The six powers of an enlightened one are the power to see forms without being blocked, to hear sounds without being blocked, to smell odors without being blocked, to taste flavors without being blocked, to feel things without being blocked, to be in the realm of phenomena without touching anything, like a reflection in a mirror.

When the mind is one with space, one is called an unobstructed wayfarer with the six powers. A scripture says, "It is even better to give to a single unminding wayfarer than to all the buddhas of past, present, and future." People who practice the Buddha Way study this path. They have no further use for wonders.

Although it is true that some Zen masters were known to have supernormal powers such as foresight and mind reading, nevertheless the general policy was to conceal these things because of the exaggerated reactions of greed and fear that they easily arouse. Shōsan's description of the "six powers of an enlightened one" is taken directly from the *Record of Rinzai,* a Chinese Zen classic influential among the Japanese Rinzai Zen schools. The Rinzai schools were those most favored by samurai interested in Zen, so this book on the Chinese founder has great prestige in Japanese Zen tradition.

This approach to "supernatural powers" undermines the very question of any argument about whether or not they exist, for two reasons. First, its underlying premise is that consciousness is itself an inconceivable miracle; in the final analysis we do not really know how we are aware, yet we are. Second, the Zen attitude towards the supernatural begins by addressing a more primary issue, the mental clarity and objectivity that would be needed to make sober sense of the whole question and its practical implications for human life.

One aspect of Shintō and Buddhist thought that has until recently seemed to Western eyes to stand on the border of the natural and supernatural, or the rational and irrational, is the sense of human kinship with animals and plants. This often reminds Christians of paganism and sorcery, to which the Church long stood opposed in all of its European territories and New World colonies.

To Buddhists of the Far East, on the other hand, it seemed unreasonably subjective and arbitrary to believe, as Christians apparently did, that humans had the only real souls among living beings. This was a logical step from saying that there was no living spirit in the natural world, but it was unconvincing to those who did not see the sense of the original premise to begin with. Recently the growing perception of ecological crisis in the West has given a new respectability to these Shintō-Buddhist sentiments of continuity, at least in terms of their psychological implications for the relationship of human technologies to life in general.

Zen master Shōsan brings up the contrast between Japanese and European concepts in terms of the distinction between animal and human souls posited by Christian belief, but it is not that he dwells on this specific point. Instead the issue leads to questioning the Christian doctrine of the eternal human soul, the reasoning behind the creation of immortal souls that could be evil and therefore damned to eternal suffering. The idea of compassion is so fundamental to Buddhism that the Christian judgment seemed cruel and merciless. Shōsan compares the Christian idea of soul with that of a Hindu system, which he considers superior to Christianity but inferior to Buddhism.

6. According to what I hear, the Christians say that animals have no real soul, so their souls die when their bodies die. Human beings, on the other hand, have added to them a true soul created by Deus, so even when their bodies die their souls do not die: depending on their good and bad deeds in this life, their souls experience pain and pleasure. For those who have done good deeds, he made a world of unending pleasure called Paradise, and sends their souls there. For those who have done bad deeds, he made a world of pain called Inferno, and sends their souls there to torture them.

If he created distinct souls in animals and humans, why did he also create evil minds in the souls of humans and cast them into hell? If this is true, it means that human damnation is entirely the work of Deus.

When Gautama Buddha appeared in the world, unliberated religion and philosophy were flourishing in India. They had immense knowledge and proposed all sorts of views. Some of their logic resembled Buddha's, but as long as their own eyes were not clear it was only talk.

The Sankhya philosophy set up twenty-five realities, with which they defined everything in the world. The first reality was called the unknown reality. Although it is before the division of heaven and earth, not in the province of good and bad, inaccessible to sensation, perception, or cognition, and therefore impossible to really name, it is nevertheless called the unknown. This unknown reality is eternal, unaffected by birth, subsistance, change, and extinction.

The twenty-fifth reality is called the reality of the spiritual self. This is named the mind of mortal man, what has been called the spirit or soul. This is also said to be eternal.

In between these two eternal realities are twenty-three other realities, which are the appearances of the world's changes, such as good and bad, fortune and calamity. These are called compounded phenomena.

When the spiritual self produces differentiated appearances, the unknown reality transmutes to manifest their forms; therefore the changes in the composition of the world are due to the arising of feelings in the spiritual self. When the spiritual self does not give rise to any feelings and returns to the unknown reality, the transformation of composite phenomena ceases forever, and the bliss of the uncreate is spontaneously realized. They say that even though the physical body decays and dies, the spiritual self does not perish, just as the master of a house leaves when the house burns down.

Philosophers with views like this expounded various systems of reasoning, but when they eventually faced the Buddha they understood their own essence directly and all became Buddha's disciples. Now these Christians do not even come close to reaching the level of the unliberated Hindus, and yet they think their doctrine is the truth. They are truly frogs in a well [who do not know how wide the sky really is].

The idea of rewards and punishments in an afterlife was not at all foreign to Japanese Buddhists. What was alien to them was the ultimate finality of the reward or punishment. The linear model of Christian time, in which a soul had one chance on earth for eternal salvation or eternal damnation, contrasted sharply with the circular model of Buddhist time, which allowed for a transpersonal and transgenerational vision of human destiny.

In the Buddhist view there was a broader range of opportunities for salvation from the fate of the soul astray than the dogmatic threat-and-promise religion the Portuguese missionaries seemed to offer. Therefore Shōsan again concludes by accusing the Christians of narrowminded bigotry, using the familiar Taoist image of the frog at the bottom of a well who believes that the opening at the mouth of the well is the whole extent of the sky.

In the final essay, Shōsan gets down to the political roots of the whole battle of polemic between the European Christians and the Shintō-Buddhist Japanese. He portrays the missionary front as destructive and deceptive, but he also fully blames the Japanese followers for empowering them. Shōsan condemns the Japanese Christian martyrs much as the modern Japanese do in saying *Damasareta hō ga warui* ("The deceived were wrong") when people have been swindled—that is, when people have been persuaded to pursue vainly high hopes, and then have not only lost out themselves but have in their haste also caused a lot of trouble to others *(meiwaku o kaketa)* on account of their own desires.

7. The Padres and their ilk who have been coming here in recent years have no fear of the Way of Heaven: making up their own Creator of the Universe, they have destroyed Shintō shrines and Buddhist temples, fooling people with all kinds of vain talk, as part of a scheme whereby Portugal will take over Japan.

   Thieving bonzes in this country cooperated, calling themselves Irmao-Padre, dragging in numerous others. They said that the buddhas of of this country are not buddhas, that the sun and moon are base matter without spiritual luminescence. Their crimes were very serious, and could not avoid the punishment of Heaven, the punishment of buddhas, the punishment of spirits, and the punishment of humanity. They have all been strung up and killed.

   The fault for this fills the chests of those who followed them. I don't know how many thousands have died. This was brought about by magic, and is not a political sanction by our government. They usurped the Way of Heaven, constructed fabrications, and led countless people to hell; the fact is evident that they ultimately brought on their own destruction by their evil, perverse, and unprincipled deeds.

   If those Padres became true illuminists, to kill even one of them would mean being cursed by the Way of Heaven. Countless Christians have been executed in this country, but what curse has there been? No matter how many times they come here, as long as the Way of Heaven exists, they will undoubtedly destroy themselves. You should know the logic of this.

Although Shōsan winds up on a decidedly Shintoistic note in spite of his main Buddhist interest, this is nevertheless represented as a reaction to foreign aggression, not simply automatic native xenophobia. So great was the Western threat to Japan, in fact, as perceived by the Shogunate, that Europe was almost completely shut out of Japan— intellectually, commercially, and politically—for some two hundred years after Shōsan wrote this anti-Christian tract in the seventeenth century. The Japanese feeling of being put upon by aggressive Western powers was not changed by the manner in which relations were reopened in the nineteenth century at the insistence of the United States, which threatened to use force if the doors of Japan were not opened to trade.

In spite of vast differences in scale, there are some ways in which relations between Japan and the West are not much more advanced than they were one hundred years ago, or even three hundred years ago. This is exemplified by the persistent vision of "sides" that think they are opposed to one another, and the structures of interaction that emerge from this vision. From a Buddhist point of view, it makes little sense to think along the conventional lines of international competition and conflict when it is not a people or a system as such but the alliance of ignorance, greed, and aggression that is the same problem everywhere. This perspective may prove to be the only viable avenue beyond the emotionally destabilizing influence of current anti-Japanese feelings in the West and parallel anti-Western feelings in Japan.

A ZEN RAZOR

While historical connections undoubtedly exist between Zen Buddhism and Japanese martial arts, their spiritual link has quite obviously never been complete. The attempt to use the historical association to imbue martial arts themselves with the dignity of Buddhism may very well be a prime example of the classical art of strategic misdirection. It may seem odd, therefore, that in spite of the widely acknowledged influence of Zen on Japanese culture and personality, virtually no critical study of Zen in modern Japan has ever been made.

A review of academic and sectarian work on Zen Buddhism quickly brings to light one central fact: that the stock of direct information on this subject is extremely limited and fragmentary. This information gap, furthermore, does not exist only in the realm of the classics, but even in what can be learned about modern Japanese Zen from easily accessible sources where the language barrier is considerably less than that presented by the classics. Some reasons for this are not far to seek, being visible in the narrow scope of sectarian and academic specializations.

Political or social reasons for selective study may also strike roots at various levels, from special interest groups to unconscious policies in public education. The barriers of knowledge and understanding do not exist, in any case, because the average Westerner is not intelligent enough to understand Zen, Japan, or the Japanese language; or because the average Japanese is not intelligent enough to understand Christianity, the West, or Western languages.

By now it has at least become a fashionable courtesy to give all humanity credit for a certain degree of basic intelligence, but it would seem imperative to examine the question of whether that courtesy is going to be used to avoid or to confront the whole issue of ignorance, its existence and operation. From a Buddhist perspective, this is a problem that is universal and exists on every side of cultural, racial, and even personal boundaries of identity. Therefore it is by attacking the central cause of the problem, and not the particular parties caught up in it, that the original Zen method of social criticism evolved outside of politics as ordinarily understood.

Zen in the classical sense involved reaching beyond the limits of insular habits so rigidly held that people can no longer use the brains they were born with. In this sense it makes little difference, in the final analysis, whether the culture is Japanese or German, English or American, or whatever it may be. The Zen question is why we feel a need to cling automatically to these presumed limitations of thinking. This was always the Zen question, and it cannot be less so today when the necessity of seeing things globally has never been more openly evident.

The transmission of knowledge about Zen and Japanese culture to the West is a topic whose importance reaches far beyond the realms of intellectual history and religious adventurism, because of needs created by political and economic relations in the modern world. This subject has been studied to some extent, but without data needed for critical analysis, which would have to consider what has not been transmitted as well as what has, and what has been accurately transmitted as compared with what has been distorted in the process.

The undeniable connection between Zen and Bushidō has come to be so taken for granted that it has been attributed to their natures as well as their histories. The distinctions between them are often not clearly defined in books on Oriental martial arts, which like their counterparts on Oriental cultural arts tend to emphasize their connection with Buddhist principles rather than the historical and ideological idiosyncrasies of their development. An examination of relevant primary literature makes it clear, however, that Bushidō is spiritually and pragmatically different from Buddhism, even if some of its practitioners did learn something about Buddhism and apply it to their arts.

The participation of warriors and strategists in shaping the format of Zen in Japan is one way to explain the cloud of mystery surrounding Zen, as the appearance of a ruse, part of the *art of the advantage,* one that has historically been used to dress certain alien and un-Buddhist elements of Bushidō in the dignity of Buddhism. Many Japanese themselves have unknowingly been deceived by this maneuver, to say nothing of Westerners.

The aspects of Japanese culture with which it is most difficult for the average Westerner to sympathize generally are derived not from

Buddhism but from Shintō; and it is these very elements that also tend to alienate the Japanese from non-Japanese in their own thoughts. Therefore if one were to look critically at the subject of Zen influence on Japanese culture and Western civilization, one would have to examine with particular care those items that mark Shintō thinking, are thoroughly out of character with Buddhist Zen, yet nevertheless are perceived as part of Japanese Zen.

The Shintoistic elements that have infected Zen over the centuries may be briefly stated as follows: fetishism, including ritualism and attachment to paraphernalia; devotion to persons living or dead; fondness for rice wine, a sacramental libation in Shintō worship; hierarchy and authoritarianism; a tendency to regard the physical body as real; racism; and local sectarianism.

Another feature found in modern Japanese Zen that is neither Buddhistic nor Shintoistic is misogyny, which has been noted in Japanese culture in general, where it might be expected as a consequence of eight centuries of military rule. This quirk is clearly derived from state Confucianism and militarism, not Buddhism or Shintō, but it is so commonly associated with Zen that it needs to be singled out for analysis before any appreciation of authentic Zen in the classical spiritual sense can be realized.

In this connection, it can also be observed that militarism has left its effects on the emotional and sexual life of the Japanese as well, subsurface tensions that are also sometimes associated with the rigors of Zen, but really derive from the attitudes of the samurai soldiers who bent Zen to their own purposes. Even today, in the highly erotic mass media of Japan, sexual intercourse can be portrayed as something inherently very much like rape; and love is ordinarily depicted as inevitably clashing with duty.

These attitudes, which are among those that generally tend to disturb Westerners and affect their views of Japanese psychology, are leftovers of eight centuries of martial rule and have nothing to do with the spirit of Buddhism. Classical Japanese literature suggests that the Japanese were far more comfortable with their tender emotions and erotic feelings before the soldiers took over in the twelfth century. One of the first things the military government did at that time was to suppress left-hand Tantra, a form of Buddhism in which sensual media such as art, song, and erotic ceremony were used as means of awakening hidden powers in the mind.

Several symptoms of alienation of the sexes, all commonly noted by observers of Japan, are linked to this militaristic suppression that began in earnest eight centuries ago: simultaneously stimulated and repressed sexuality, a resulting undercurrent of violence, and acute manifestations of these phenomena in the form of sadomasochism, are quite evidently products of extended military domination. Similar phenomena can be seen in all societies when they are in militaristic phases of their development.

It is no coincidence that the *I Ching,* China's classic *Book of Change,* for thousands of years one of the most prestigious guides to statecraft in the Orient, contains warnings against assumption of civil rule by military men. The negative effects of eight hundred years of samurai rule in Japan would seem to bear witness to the soundness of this ancient caveat.

Militarism has distorted Zen along with the rest of Japanese culture, producing aberrations in which various forms of Japanese machismo or masochism are regarded as not only having some relation to Zen, but even as being products or manifestations of Zen "practice" or "realization." Furthermore, Japanese people today are just as susceptible to being deceived by deviant Zen as are Westerners, with the result that the various conflicting elements in modern Zen are generally not analyzed for what they really are. Perhaps the burden of ignoring these conflicts is the reason why contemporary Zen in Japan generally does not reflect robustness or optimism, and why it does not seem to influence the culture any longer in a fundamental way.

Institutional Zen Buddhism in contemporary Japan is often accused of being moribund even by its own monastic inmates and literary exponents, to say nothing of outside critics. Various facets of this sluggishness are widely acknowledged in Japanese Zen literature, but their fundamental causes are seldom rooted out, nor are they discussed very frankly in Zen for export. The commercialization of Zen in the West, plus the exploitation of Western interest in Zen or Zen-derived cultural forms in efforts to enhance Japan's image, have militated against unbiased information and objective appraisal.

Therefore the philia-phobia polarity in Western thinking about Japan has not been reduced as much as it could have been by the undoubtedly active interest in Zen and Japanese culture existing in the West today, had the transcendental and cultural aspects of this interest been clearly distinguished and funded with adequate exposure to information about the essential meaning of Zen and about historical institutions established at various times in Japan for the overt purpose of studying or otherwise upholding Zen.

One of the forms of Japanese culture that appears to be strongly influenced by certain aspects of Bushidō-Zen and that calls for critical examination in the contemporary West is the *jigoku* ("hell") style of training used in Japanese education and personnel development. Since Westerners have to deal with the results of this kind of training, and attempts are also underway to import it to the West, there is a distinct need for critical examination of its reality.

Several years ago, something of a stir was created by the suicide of one of the most respected Zen masters in Japan, who was at that time both abbot and spiritual director of a monastery traditionally ranked in the very highest echelon of Rinzai Zen. Various opinions as to the reasons for his suicide were put forth, including ill health, but his own book, *Takuan ishi no satori*, "The Enlightenment of a Pickle-Pressing Stone," contains some very negative observations of Zen and contemporary Japanese life.

Among them are the abbot's views on the use of Zen training to make people stronger and tougher for getting along in the business world, a practice he calls *fuzaketa*, a word meaning ludicrous, or, in a relational context, having the characteristic of mere dalliance or sport. In the West there is also a strong undercurrent of shortsightedness in both academic and popular interest in Zen, which has been relegated to cult status even within their own spheres of interest, and thus treated in a fragmentary and idiosyncratic manner in Western culture as a whole.

Whenever anti-Japanese feeling among Western nations reaches a certain pitch, there is a renewal of the popular Japanese myth that Westerners would feel more kindly disposed to Japan if they understood Japanese culture. The West cannot afford to be mystified by the mystery of Japan, or to allow information to be used as a weapon in what Musashi calls the *art of the advantage*. There are those who glamorize Japan and seem to feel that the West should try to imitate its ways; there are others who vilify Japan and apparently regard it as a menace. Both extremes are casualties of *the art of war*, who in turn victimize others to the extent of their own influence.

One of the main problems faced by both Japan and the West is the intimate connection between special interests and the dissemination of information and knowledge. This is a two-way street, because racist misperceptions and political projections always work together to the detriment of public understanding. The real enemy on either side is ignorance, whether it be natural or contrived.

One of the characteristic marks of ignorance is blind prejudice, and it is useful to watch out for it when assessing subjective reactions to perceptions of attitudes. In the matter of martial arts, militarism, and their influence on human society, the question of function is paramount in the formation of classical philosophy. The Japanese martial arts were more or less transformed into therapeutic and performing arts during the long Pax Tokugawa, which began in the early seventeenth century and lasted some two hundred and fifty years, until the American *Black Ships* threatened to "huff, puff, and blow their house down" if the Japanese didn't let them into Japan in the mid-nineteenth century.

In the first century of the long peace, the development of various competing schools of martial arts formed a relatively harmless channel for male aggression and ambition left over from the bloody *Sengoku jidai,* Era of the Warring States, a hundred years of constant strife. Furthermore, while this remaining violence was thereby largely vented away from government and society into private groups, the ancient Zen connections of Bushidō also exposed the martially inclined to the Buddhist philosophy of self-mastery, and occasionally to Buddhist ethics as well. In the Tantric Buddhist idiom, such use of "instruments of ill omen" to achieve a worthy purpose is called "using a thorn to extract a thorn."

Oriental martial arts are to some extent performing a similar function in urban American society today. This is undoubtedly one of their most rational adaptations, as it was in Japan of the seventeenth century. Over the next hundred years in Japan, however, the growing number and discontent of disenfranchised samurai rekindled some deadly flames. Martial prowess could (as ever) be used for wantonly criminal purposes; and the line between chivalrous competition and political violence was easily overstepped in the name of Bushidō.

In the nineteenth century, the breaking of Japanese isolation fostered diametrically opposed movements in Bushidō, just as they did in Zen Buddhism. On the one hand, through renewed contact with China, certain modern Japanese pioneers took an interest in Taoist martial arts and developed more peaceful, unarmed Japanese martial arts. On the other hand, through confrontation with the aggressive, well-armed West, militaristic factions of Bushidō turned to Spartan training designed to make the entire being, mind and body, into a weapon.

The "soft" martial arts are generally favored by people interested in the spiritual tradition of Zen, while the "hard" martial arts are favored by the police, armed forces, and *jigoku* ("hell") training systems in education, business, and industry. There are also any number of shades in between these extremes, but it is in most concentrated form that their peculiar characteristics, including their specific functions and side effects, can be most clearly seen.

Therefore a stark examination of primitive elements can be construed as prejudicial by the already prejudiced, but it is as impossible to understand a composite without understanding its parts as it is impossible to understand the parts without understanding them as parts of a whole.

SUMMARY

Crucial to understanding Japanese psychology and behavior is an assessment of the influence of centuries of military rule. The development of economic, political, social, and educational structures of Japan reflects this influence, ingrained into the nation through the elevation of the samurai caste into a political and moral elite over a period of hundreds of years.

Warfare in Japan was originally the domain of aristocratic clans. These clans believed themselves to be descended from one of three sources: they thought they were direct descendants of deities, direct descendants of ancient emperors of Japan, or direct descendants of Chinese or Korean nobility. The imperial clan is one of the first category, those believed to be directly descended from deities. This particular clan is associated with the goddess of the sun, who was assigned precedence in the Shintō pantheon with the rise of this clan and its allies in ancient Japan. Their mythology is the basis of state Shintō, the imperial version of native Japanese religion.

The connections with Korea and China maintained by the powerful Japanese clans enabled them to develop the arms with which they asserted political dominance. In their mythology, the sword is one of the symbols of the imperial family of the sun goddess clan, and the process of sword making has traditionally been associated with Shintō. Sword fetishism, eventually to become a characteristic exaggeration of Bushidō, reflects an element of primitive Shintō in the psychology of the samurai.

Territorial conflicts continued even after the allies of the sun goddess clan established a national Japanese state on the Chinese model around 600 C.E. Genocidal warfare against the other peoples inhabiting those islands also continued. Frontier wars and clan competition among the Japanese themselves stimulated the development of a separate military caste, descended from the old aristocracy but with its own distinct history and heritage. This new caste also produced the stewards, marshals, and sheriffs engaged by upper-class landowners in the capital to manage and police their far-flung estates. Eventually the military men demanded more for their services, and the first centralized martial paragovernment was set up in 1185. This was the beginning of the Bakufu "Tent Government" of the Shogunate.

Three military regimes dominated Japanese society and politics from 1185 to 1868. Two more martial regimes have appeared since but have ruled in the name of the emperor rather than the Shōgun. The first two Shogunates patronized Zen Buddhism, breaking with the established Buddhist schools whose churches were all run by members of the old aristocracy. The third Shogunate patronized Confucianism and attempted to divide and repress Buddhism. The fourth martial regime openly suppressed Buddhism in the late nineteenth and early twentieth centuries, in the name of Shintō nationalism. The fifth martial regime forced Buddhist churches into an alliance with state Shintō during the second quarter of the twentieth century.

Zen Buddhist elements in the Japanese warrior code originally came from the time when Zen became fashionable among samurai clans through the encouragement of the Shōguns. Neo-Confucianism was also passed on to the warriors by early Zen Buddhists, but it was probably not until the establishment of Neo-Confucianism as state orthodoxy in the seventeenth century that this element came to predominate in the samurai codes of Bushido.

All Japanese traditions were codified during the era of the last Shogunate, except for Bushidō, which was written in some way into house rules for clans and organizations, but never unified or finalized. There are Shintō, Buddhist, Taoist, Confucian, Legalist, and militarist elements to be found in various representations of Bushidō, but no generalizations as to their proportion in an abstract "Bushido" may be made, except on the level where concrete facts are evident to common view in the light of history. This may reflect the inherently competitive nature of the art of war, the deliberate vagueness of the art of the advantage, in which anything might be set forward according to the convenience of the time.

This volume explores the relationship between Zen Buddhism and the samurai cult of Bushido through the works of four distinguished authors, two Zen masters and two martial artists. The popular idea of Zen spirituality in the martial arts is examined critically with a view to discerning the discontinuity as well as the continuity between these two facets of Japanese culture. The connection is considered from two points of view: Zen influence on the way of the warrior, and the influence of militarism on the development of Japanese Zen.

The four authors whose works form the bones of this book represent several distinct types among those involved in Zen and the martial arts. Zen master Takuan elucidates the essence of Zen mindfulness as it applies to the way of the warrior. The swordsman Yagyū Munenori applies the ethics and psychology of Zen to martial arts. Zen master Suzuki Shōsan demonstrates the spirit of warriorhood in the practice of Zen. Miyamoto Musashi the duelist represents the warlike strategy of militarist using Zen techniques without Buddhist ethics.

In Takuan's work on the immutable mind, there is no express morality. Yagyū applies Zen to martial arts but subordinates martial arts to the service of political morality. Shōsan uses the psychology of the warrior in the art of Zen self-mastery; he is both technical and ethical, going further than Takuan and Yagyū in depth and extension. Musashi is not as clear as the more spiritual Zennists; he may have been trying to use the warrior's way to master himself, but it looks like that way got the better of him. Musashi shows a warlike spirit appearing to be ultimately devoted neither to Zen enlightenment nor to social morality but only to the perfection of his art in itself, which embodies the quest for victory as the supreme goal. It does not seem odd that Musashi surpasses the others in the ruthlessness of his strategy and appears to fall short of the others in Buddhist understanding; yet his dedication, discipline, and winning record still pass for admirable things in themselves.

None of these types alone may be taken to represent a general picture of Japanese culture and psychology as they are manifested in those areas influenced by Zen or militarism over the centuries. All of them are present in various proportions, sometimes even within the same individual. Interactive confusion and misunderstanding often result from failure to distinguish the different aspects of Zen and martialism as they actually operate in various mixtures.

There is an inside (ura) and an outside (omote) to every form of Japanese culture. Matters of "face" are therefore as important as matters of substance in social, business, or political interactions. What is outwardly made most visible of any form of Japanese culture, whether it be Zen, martial arts, or any other facet of that civilization, normally consists of the most commercialized and/or politicized versions, not necessarily the most refined or authentic. The obvious front is not the measure of what it is supposed to represent, even though the existence of the facades is an inescapable fact of life when dealing with Japanese culture as a political reality. As an aspect of strategic maneuvering, the commercialized and politicized outward forms of culture belong to the category of Japanese behavior deriving from the "art of the advantage" developed by martialists.

The substitution of overgeneralizations and clichés for authentic information and critical analysis is itself a common "art of war." Its use to pit the emotions of nations and cultures against one another is also an art of war, one that camouflages an underlying opposition of a different nature. It is the impersonal insight that marked original noncultural Zen Buddhism, and not the kind of superficial intercultural understanding that confuses the surface with the interior, that can distinguish this fundamental opposition between those who exploit ignorance and those in need of knowledge.

INDEX

SHAMBHALA CLASSICS

Appreciate Your Life: The Essence of Zen Practice, by Taizan Maezumi Roshi.

The Art of Peace, by Morihei Ueshiba. Edited by John Stevens.

The Art of War, by Sun Tzu. Translated by the Denma Translation Group.

The Art of Worldly Wisdom, by Baltasar Gracián. Translated by Joseph Jacobs.

The Book of Five Rings, by Miyamoto Musashi. Translated by Thomas Cleary.

The Book of Tea, by Kakuzo Okakura.

Breath by Breath: The Liberating Practice of Insight Meditation, by Larry Rosenberg.

The Buddha and His Teachings. Edited by Samuel Bercholz and Sherab Chödzin Kohn.

The Diamond Sutra and The Sutra of Hui-neng. Translated by Wong Mou-lam and A. F. Price.

The Eight Gates of Zen: A Program of Zen Training, by John Daido Loori.

The Great Path of Awakening, by Jamgon Kongtrul. Translated by Ken McLeod.

Insight Meditation: A Psychology of Freedom, by Joseph Goldstein.

The Japanese Art of War: Understanding the Culture of Strategy, by Thomas Cleary.

Kabbalah: The Way of the Jewish Mystic, by Perle Epstein.

Lovingkindness: The Revolutionary Art of Happiness, by Sharon Salzberg.

Meditations, by J. Krishnamurti.

Monkey: A Journey to the West, by David Kherdian.

The Myth of Freedom and the Way of Meditation, by Chögyam Trungpa.

Narrow Road to the Interior and Other Writings, by Matsuo Bashō. Translated by Sam Hamill.

The Rumi Collection: An Anthology of Translations of Mevlâna Jalâluddin Rumi. Edited by Kabir Helminski.

Seeking the Heart of Wisdom: The Path of Insight Meditation, by Joseph Goldstein and Jack Kornfield.

Seven Taoist Masters: A Folk Novel of China. Translated by Eva Wong.

Siddhartha, by Hermann Hesse. Translated by Sherab Chödzin Kohn.

Spiritual Teaching of Ramana Maharshi, by Ramana Maharshi.

Start Where You Are: A Guide to Compassionate Living, by Pema Chödrön.

T'ai Chi Classics. Translated with commentary by Waysun Liao.

The Tibetan Book of the Dead: The Great Liberation through Hearing in the Bardo. Translated with commentary by Francesca Fremantle and Chögyam Trungpa.

Training the Mind and Cultivating Loving-Kindness, by Chögyam Trungpa.

The Tree of Yoga, by B. K. S. Iyengar.

The Way of the Bodhisattva, by Shantideva. Translated by the Padmakara Translation Group.

The Way of a Pilgrim and The Pilgrim Continues His Way. Translated by Olga Savin.

When Things Fall Apart: Heart Advice for Difficult Times, by Pema Chödrön.

The Wisdom of No Escape and the Path of Loving-Kindness, by Pema Chödrön.

The Wisdom of the Prophet: Sayings of Muhammad. Translated by Thomas Cleary.

The Yoga-Sūtra of Patañjali: A New Translation with Commentary. Translated by Chip Hartranft.

Zen Lessons: The Art of Leadership. Translated by Thomas Cleary.